A Hunter's Field Notes

JAY HOUSTON
ROGER MEDLEY

HARVEST HOUSE PUBLISHERS

EUGENE, OREGON

A HUNTER'S FIELD NOTES
Copyright 2012 by Jay Houston and Roger Medley
Published by Harvest House Publishers
Eugene, Oregon 97402
www.harvesthousepublishers.com

Library of Congress Cataloging-in-Publication Data
Houston, Jay, 1953–
A hunter's field notes / Jay Houston and Roger Medley.
p. cm.
Includes bibliographical references.
ISBN 978-0-7369-4364-2 (pbk.)
ISBN 978-0-7369-4366-6 (eBook)
1. Christian men—Religious life. 2. Hunting—Religious aspects—Christianity. I. Medley, Roger, 1961– . II. Title.
BV4597.4H68 2012
248.8'42—dc23
2011038141

Acknowledgments

We want to give any glory for this project to God. Were it not for the sometimes gentle and other times not so gentle leading of His Holy Spirit, this book would never have seen the light of day. His gentle leading came in the form of many phone calls where "what is God saying to you?" and "really? Me too" were the topics.

Authors write books for all sorts of reasons; however, in this case we agreed we were only God's tools and He wanted to do something much bigger than the two of us. In *A Hunter's Field Notes,* God has used some of the stories that have come from our travels along our life trails as well as lessons learned along the way that will speak to men who, like us, love the hunting life and the outdoors.

Our prayer is that if this book makes a positive difference in your life you will do two things: give God the glory and pass the book along to a family member or friend.

We want to thank our good friend and fellow hunting buddy Steve Chapman for his encouragement and for opening the publishing door, our editor Barb Gordon for her amazing skill with words and loving patience, and Harvest House acquisitions editor Terry Glaspey for taking a chance on us.

Jay
Roger

An Opportunity for You
by Steve Chapman

Through the years I've received some very inspiring and encouraging letters from individuals who have read the hunting books I've written, including *A Look at Life from a Deer Stand*. But there's one letter that will always remain among the most unforgettable. It was from a young man who knew his dad loved him supremely, but because his father was not the kind to verbalize his thoughts, the young man was resigned to the likelihood that he would never hear them.

Then one day the son got the heartbreaking news that his dad had suddenly died. All hope was lost that he would ever know what sentiments filled his father's heart. That is, until the day he found one of my books with some handwritten notes on the open spaces inside the front cover. They were from his father's pen and written for his son's heart. The young man wept as he read the words. He could almost hear his dad's voice in the writing that revealed his father's carefully chosen expressions of love and appreciation for his son. There is no way to measure the depth of joy the son felt. And I was moved to tears when the son shared his story with me and sent scans of his dad's writing.

When Jay Houston and Roger Medley mentioned the idea of creating a book called *A Hunter's Field Notes* that focused on passing down thoughts and hunting lore as legacies, I immediately remembered the young man's story. I thought of how many sons, as well as dads, moms, husbands, wives, and other family members and friends, might someday be deeply touched by reading the thoughts from the hearts of people they love. For that reason, I'm thrilled this book idea has become a reality.

When you get into *A Hunter's Field Notes,* you'll find it is much more than just ink on paper. It is your opportunity to create a priceless heirloom—one that contains the incredibly valuable gems of the feelings that fill your soul. Keep in mind that as you write on the pages, you'll be blessing those who come behind you in time and encouraging those who continue on after your hunting days are over.

Steve Chapman

Contents

Two Trails, One Destination

[Isaac said to Esau,] "Now then, get your equipment—your quiver and bow—and go out to the open country to hunt some wild game for me. Prepare me the kind of tasty food I like and bring it to me to eat, so that I may give you my blessing" (Genesis 27:3-4).

The original concept of creating an easy-to-do journaling guide for those who love the outdoors came years ago when Roger and I first met over breakfast at a Cracker Barrel restaurant in Colorado Springs. *A Hunter's Field Notes* is the result of nearly three decades of personal journaling and prayer, along with a collaborative collection of high-country and backwoods stories, biblical parallels, lessons learned, and personal encouragement extracted from two separate yet Christ-centered lifetimes. As a team, Roger and I pledged to remain loyal to one imperative: to only write as God's Holy Spirit inspired and directed us. After nearly a year of prayerful writing, we got together to combine our respective efforts. It became clear that while we originally thought it would all blend together into one voice, so to speak, God clearly had something else in mind: two distinct trails leading to the same destination.

We invite you to journey into the hunter's woods with us, moving along the separate trails that we pray and believe will give you plenty of insights, encouragement, and know-how to preserve your own thoughts and stories for the generations to come.

A Hunter's Field Notes is a "how to" book cloaked within the stories and adventures of two hunters. Our hope is that our tales will call to mind similar stories from your own experiences. We pray the gently probing questions in the "Your Field Notes" sections will help you record your own adventures. We encourage you to put down your thoughts. Even if you only jot down a few lines in each section, that's a good start. Based on our experiences, each time a person writes his thoughts and shares his stories, it gets a little easier.

So tighten up your boots, put on your backpack, grab your rifle or bow, and let's hit the trail with God. We have a few miles to go before it gets dark.

Part 1

Jay's Trail

Introduction
by Jay Houston

Years ago I made a friend who has since become my best friend and full-time hunting companion. When I try to recall the memory from that first time we spent together, I remember that he wasn't an aggressive or assertive person like so many guys I was used to hanging out with. He was more reflective and encouraging, and I liked that. Since that first meeting, our friendship has grown from that of strangers to buddies, then to family friend, and on to best friend. Unlike so many who spend time talking about themselves, this guy always seemed interested in talking more about me than him. In the world I lived in at the time, that was rare.

Somewhere along our journey together—I think it was in the early 1970s, I wondered, *What is it about this man that is so affable?* The answer was not long in coming. I realized that unlike a lot of folks, this guy actually cared about my life.

Over the years, he and I have traveled many trails together. I know and love his family and he loves mine as if it were his own. When my first marriage broke up, he was there as a comforter and friend. When I lost my job, again he was right there beside me offering words of encouragement. When some people hurled stones of hate against me, he drew closer than ever—like a father protecting his child. I had never known anyone like this (especially a guy). One day when I couldn't stand it any longer, I asked, "How much do you really care about me?"

His countenance appeared somewhat worn by age but his eyes spar-kled like jewels in the morning sun. He smiled and responded, "Jay, I love you so much! I gave up my own family, including my one and only child, that you might have life and the opportunity to live it to its fullest."

"You did that for me?" I asked.

"Yes, just for you," he said with a hint of a grin as he stood there.

I didn't know what to do or what to say. With my heart almost bursting out of my chest I asked, "How can I repay You, God? What can I do?"

He answered, "Jay, you can't repay Me, but you can *do* something for Me. The love I've shown you, the passion I've endowed you with, the lessons I've allowed you to learn—write them down. Pass them on. They are your legacy. Tell others of the trails you and I have traveled together. Share with them the stories of joy and sorrow. Tell them of the victories and the challenges we've faced together. All of these have made you who you are. Tell them what a great team we make. All these years and all these trails have prepared you to become exactly the per-son I created you to be from the very beginning of time. By telling 'our story,' you will be telling My story. You will be honoring Me. And, Jay," He added, "tell them I am here for them too. If they want to get My attention, they just need to call My name. I'm always listening."

Friends, this book is the first volume of that story. This is first and foremost a book of encouragement…gently prodding you to tell your story so your family and future generations will have the opportunity to know you better and learn from you. My heartfelt prayer is that this book will bless your life—and that your life will bless others. Tell your story…your legacy. Pass it on.

If you need a little motivation, consider this: The Bible is the best-selling book of all time. It has impacted and changed more lives than any other book ever written. God, through His Holy Spirit, inspired men to write down their stories to encourage, teach, and admonish us. And in a small way, He lets us do the same in the lives of the people we love, know, and interact with—even extending to future generations.

1

Encouragement
for Every Hunter

Hunters and outdoorsmen like you enjoy a challenge and love the thrill of pursuing a worthy adversary. You find pleasure and solace in experiencing adventures found only in wild country far from the sounds and smells of cities and humanity. You prefer to smell the aroma of wood smoke rising from a campfire to that of exhaust while stuck in traffic. You probably spend more hours than you care to admit shivering in a treestand overlooking a stand of hardwoods or a food plot you worked tirelessly on all summer. You take pleasure in crouching in a cramped, dark, ground blind awaiting a glimpse of a trophy buck that the smoky-gray light of dawn might reveal. Or maybe you prefer hiking mile-high ridgelines in pursuit of backcountry ghosts, such as mule deer and elk. Just hearing the words "hunting season," "deer," "elk," and "turkey" stirs something deep within your soul, causing an unexpected rush of adrenalin. A chill runs up your spine and perhaps your trigger finger involuntarily moves just a bit. Sound familiar? Does this hit home with you? Have you ever been told you're addicted to hunting or to the outdoors? If so, this book is for you. Read on, brother!

Nearly every fall for more than 30 years, my good friend and cowriter Roger Medley and I have headed out for wild places after loading into our trucks or SUVs our tents, sleeping bags, food, and more "gotta have it" gear than most men will ever really need. Most of our hunting trips have meant wives, sons, and daughters are left behind.

While Rog and I have not always hunted together, we have each journeyed to remote wilderness places to spend days and sometimes weeks fulfilling a primeval urge to engage wild game on their own ground in hopes of a harvest.

Some years the hunting trail ends with high fives followed by backstraps on the grill. Don't you love "tag" soup? Other trips, well, not so much excitement. I'm sure you've experienced these things too. Every hunt, every day in the wilderness, gifts us with enduring memories, unique experiences, lessons learned along the trail, nature observations, tall-tale fodder, stories of hunts told around a fire, prayers offered, and prayers answered. The essence of who we are as hunters and outdoorsmen is renewed every fall.

Unfortunately, much of that adventure, much of that essence, much of that experience is lost to our family members and friends who weren't with us, as well as future generations. I encourage you to journey along with Roger and me as we show via our stories the value of recording aspects of our lives—our legacy—to share with our offspring. Think about it. A few minutes of your time invested in this process may impact countless lives as people are touched by the knowledge of your life, loves, joys, accomplishments, thoughts, and prayers.

As you travel with us through a few of our adventures, look for intersections with your own stories. These memories may come back to you as short recollections instead of complete tales. Write them down however they come. The process of writing may trigger more memories you can add. Before long there will be dozens and dozens of memorable glimpses into your life that may reveal wisdom even you aren't aware of. These thoughts, these memories, are *your* field notes.

Gary Miller, a true brother, longtime deer and turkey hunter, author of *Outdoor Truths,* and an awesome man of God, shared these insights with me recently that I think will further encourage you to consider leaving a written legacy:

> Writing allows us to do at least three things. First, it allows us to *expand our territory*. Preaching to even a big congregation is limited. Only those who are there on that Sunday

can take in a great sermon. But the printed word moves from reader to reader and can be transferred to places we personally haven't gone to.

Second, it allows us to *extend our time*. No matter how great we may be to a congregation [or group], one day we will die. And eventually we will be mostly forgotten. Sure, our names might be etched on a plaque on some building, but unless we have written our thoughts down, death will shut our mouths forever. Writing extends a person's life, voice, influence, and ministry.

Last, it allows us to *express our truth*. Writing is a good way to be understood. It allows us to pick our subjects and linger on them. It is an opportunity to think before we speak. It allows us to pick the right words and illustrations to fully explain what we want our readers to know. It allows us to state our beliefs and doctrines and then teach without time constraints.

David's Field Notes

A twenty-first century look back at one of the rock stars of the Bible—David, the man who would become king over all of Israel—shows us…Well, what do we see? A man some today might call a train wreck. On the surface we see a person who was betrayed by his friends, hounded by the government, and a fugitive from the law. He was a voyeur, an adulterer, and a murderer. Yet God called him "a man after his own heart"! Had David not produced a written record—his "field notes"—much of his life and the lessons he learned in the crucible of life and the victories forged under fire would have been lost for all time. Can you imagine the tragedy of such a loss to mankind?

David is one of my personal heroes. His story gives me hope and encouragement. I see so many similarities in our lives. David the king chronicled his life, his dreams, his fears, his failures, and his victories for the generations to come. Many of his writings are recorded in the biblical book of Psalms. Psalm 119 is my favorite. In this psalm, we are allowed to see how David's faith in the God he could not see or touch but whom he had ongoing conversations with gave him the courage to overcome near crippling depression:

> I'm feeling terrible—I couldn't feel worse! Get me on my feet again. You promised, remember?...My sad life's dilapidated, a falling-down barn; build me up again by your Word. Barricade the road that goes Nowhere; grace me with your clear revelation. I choose the true road to Somewhere, I post your road signs at every curve and corner... I'll run the course you lay out for me if you'll just show me how (Psalm 119:25,28-30,32 msg).

I speculate that David's motivation in putting his story—his field notes—to paper may have been that he wanted a format where he could cry out to God in private, a volume where he could track his thoughts, petitions, and more so he would be aware of God's replies and guidance.

Have you been in such a place or time? Have you felt persecuted, hard pressed, set upon, hopeless? If we are honest, most of us would answer yes to most if not all of David's thoughts. Our personal journey through trying times and dealing with challenges breeds character. Someone once told me that "character is who we are when no one else is looking." I wholeheartedly agree.

When I visualize David the hunter and avid outdoorsman, I see a man's man sitting with his back to a boulder high on a mountainside. He's alone with his thoughts and with God, in a place of quiet retreat from the craziness of life. Perhaps he left his home and family long before dawn so he could be on the mountain to see the magnificence of the sunrise. David loved wild places because they offered him challenges and sanctuary.

As hunters, we too are drawn to these wild places, these sanctuaries of lodgepole pine, oak, and aspen. We dream of returning to such places all year long, yet when the time comes to camo-up and strike out for that distant treestand or mountainside overlook, we often give little deliberation to how our journey affects the lives of those we love more than anything.

From the early days of his youth, David learned that the outdoors offered him a solitude that he couldn't find in town, a retreat where he could work through some of the stress in his life he needed to deal with. Sound familiar? I believe David wanted to leave something for the future—a record for those who would come after him. So he left writings that tell of his life and the role that his loving God played in it. He wanted others to learn from his experiences. I don't think for a second that David set out to write a bestseller that would change the world. He just wrote what he thought, what he felt, what he experienced, what he prayed straight from his heart. And I, for one, am thankful for the record he left! At times my life too seems like a train wreck, and I find comfort and encouragement time and time again in David's stories.

A Hunter's Field Notes is designed to help you retain and record your memories, adventures, and perhaps milestones that might otherwise be lost in the smoke rising heavenward over a campfire. Roger and I want to assist you in sharing with your family what moves you and what is valuable to you in terms of the past as well as the future. My good friend and fellow hunter Steve Chapman makes the argument for journaling well: "Unless we leave behind a written record, the greatest portion of our life experiences, as well as the lessons learned from them along the way, are too often obscured by the passage of time. Consequently, passing along those valuable insights is threatened." Journaling gives you a forum that can help you clarify your thoughts, record your experiences and observations, work through issues and feelings, and pass along the essence of who you are in Jesus to future generations.

YOUR FIELD NOTES

Who is one of your personal heroes? Why?_

- The apostle Paul.
- He as this book states, journaling his life shy always writing his thoughts, Instructions to the various people and their NEW churches.
- Almost every far dome I Paul, "poor me, I'm in prison, suffering!!! yet the suffers so the church of Christ continued to grow!!

How has the life of this person impacted you?

- Paul makes me realize that suffering will come & being a christian, yet we know our savior will save us from the death/pain of sin.

Who do you think will be encouraged when they read your field notes?

- My son and daughter and their children.

This might be a good place to leave that person a personal note. You can't imagine how this will impact him 10 or 20 or 30 years from now. I assure you it will!

I have 2 personal heroes ; Paul - I can't leave him a message!! But I read his messages in the living word.
- My wife is my living personal hero.
- She is a God fearing, God loving wife. I'm so blessed to have her in my life.
- Everyday she is in physical pain, yet always giving her love, time without complaint. I love her so _very_ much !,

Be Prepared!

If ever I needed proof positive that every hunter needs to push beyond the fundamentals and prepare by getting as much knowledge of the game and the environment in which he's going to, my experience during a 2004 elk hunt brought it home.

Colorado's second rifle season in mid-October is a challenging time to hunt elk. The rut is over. An army of bow hunters and riflemen has assaulted the backcountry and pressured the elk from every direction imaginable since the end of August. On this particular trip, our gaggle of six hunters, beset with years of anticipation, arrived at the 10,000-foot base camp high in the Rockies about mid-afternoon on a Sunday astride tuckered out mountain horses. After almost four hours in the saddle, our backsides were numb. We managed to quickly unload our rifles and gear from the horses and decided to head for the timber just beyond camp to begin our search for the elusive Rocky Mountain branch-antlered beasts. (According to www.nationmaster.com, "the Shawnee called them *wapiti,* which means "white rump."")

Four of the first five days of some very hard hunting met us with bone-chilling temperatures, howling winds, and rain, snow, and sleet. I remember sitting on the edge of a small hidden meadow one afternoon surrounded by multiple stands of quaking aspen stripped bare of their golden fall cloaks. I was hunkered down as low as I could get—trying to stay warm, listening to the never-ending wail of the wind that seemed to be passing just over my head. I thought briefly about trying my cow elk call, but I had serious doubts that the elk could have heard a ship's foghorn in all that racket. I think you get the picture. Elk hunting was very tough. A 350-inch "Boone and Crockett" bull elk could have walked up right behind me, bugled, and I probably wouldn't have heard him!

Clearly the elk didn't care for the weather any more than our small band did because in four days of very hard hunting covering dozens of miles—that seemed mostly uphill—my guide, hunting partners, and I managed to only eyeball one young spike and a couple of cows. When the weather turns sour in the high country, as it most assuredly had this particular week, the elk dig in and wait it out.

Late in the afternoon on our fourth day of trying to pry elk out of the quakie patches and black timber of northwestern Colorado, Murphy—of the famed Murphy's Laws—reared his head in the form of a single, 20-pound, horse-eating porcupine. This critter took it upon himself to single-handedly "assault"—referencing the horse version of the story—three 1500-pound mountain horses and as many fully armed hunters. Can you visualize this picture? Three huge, fully camouflaged men armed to the teeth atop three massive horses strung out in a line about 100 feet apart and going up a trail to the top of a rocky ridge. Out strolls this little black prickly demon, more or less minding his own business. Actually, I never saw the thorny little rascal, but his presence in close proximity to our guide's horse, as innocent as it may have been, initiated a catastrophic chain of events.

While some of the details are still a bit fuzzy all these years later, I can still see the lead horse come to a decision that all was not well in her world. In what seemed like slow motion and the space of time I think was just a few seconds, all three horses, one after the other like a cascading set of dominoes, went stark-raving nuts and departed the mountain for parts unknown, depositing all three hunters on the ground in various states of disrepair.

Angel, the lead horse, had let her rider (our guide) *almost* dismount before deciding to make a beeline down the mountain. He was still removing his foot from the stirrup, so he was flipped like a cheap burger during his horse's escape. Horse two decided to begin his escape by charging headlong through a grove of aspens, like famed mountain man Jeremiah Johnson's horse did racing back to the cabin (in the movie version, at least). Most of the trees were barely far enough apart for the horse to get through, much less a horse with a large newbie rider hanging on to the saddle for dear life. Not wanting to be left out of all the drama, my mount decided he didn't want any part of whatever was going on up the trail and initiated his immediate bail out on two legs rather than four.

Friend, if you have never seen the view from the back of a horse whose front feet are high in the air over your head while pirouetting on his back legs…count yourself blessed. As my steed completed his 180-degree turn, he threw his head violently to one side pulling the reins from my hands, leaving me with no control over where he was going or what he was doing. When his front legs finally reunited with Mother Earth, all I could see were the other two now riderless horses going down the mountain like they'd been snake bit.

Not wanting to hang on to a runaway horse about to go crazy for the lead in a three-horse race down the mountain, I decided it was time to bail while I still had a vote. My less-than-graceful dismount ended when I hit the ground like a sack of bricks. For a minute or so I was still, making sure I was alive. A brief examination confirmed my fears that not all of my body parts were working as they should. After a few minutes, when the fog in my head began to clear, I could see my hunting partner, Joe, about 100 yards down the mountain. He was standing up, then falling down, then resting for a while, and then finally staggering to something remotely resembling a vertical human.

Once our guide was able to stand, he hobbled up and asked if I was okay.

With all the clarity of a coastal-morning fogbank, I told him I was alive at least but that my right arm wasn't working at all. Assuming I would survive for a few minutes (according to *his* version), he walked down the hill to see what kind of shape Joe was in. I guess he was satisfied we were both okay for the time being because he took off. Later we learned he was looking for the horses; however, at the time, neither Joe nor I had a clue where he went, when he might return, or if he would return. For what seemed like an eternity, that was the last time Joe and I saw another human being.

Like so many hunters of my generation, I grew up reading *Outdoor Life* magazine. As a youngster growing up in the South, I was fascinated by tales of terrifying grizzlies roaming the wilds of Wyoming and the majestic elk and mule deer that lived high in the rimrock and forests of the Rocky Mountains. Having been no farther west than Arkansas until I was almost a teenager, all such creatures and stories were vivid visions in a young man's dreams. One section of every issue that I always turned to first captured my attention. "This Happened to Me" was a cartoon-type feature that reenacted some disastrous event that had befallen an unfortunate outdoorsman. Whether it was an unwitting hunter stumbling upon a sow grizzly with cubs or an errant fisherman who had fallen through the ice, most stories were cases of catastrophe and survival—events where a man had to really rely on his skills, wits, and more than a fundamental knowledge of the outdoors to come out alive.

Out West it's referred to as "cowboy up." I think what attracted me to these articles the most was the fact that the victim of the unfortunate occurrences could be anyone—including me! It brought the story and the message home on a very personal level. In every story the author managed to embed some realized truth. His objective was to pass on a lesson learned to the reader in the hopes that he or she would be more aware and able to avoid the misfortune.

Such is the case in my story. While the triggering event may have been somewhat calamitous and was surely not intentional on the little porky's part, the real gems are the lessons I learned as a result and along the way.

Hunting is fraught with all manner of risks, including surprise storms, the possibility of physical injury, and even becoming disoriented in an immense and unforgiving land. Plans are generally not in place, and contingencies for the unexpected are often not discussed with fellow hunters or family. In essence, when we fail to plan for the unforeseen, we are planning to fail and setting the stage for future disasters. I was very fortunate during this elk hunt that my injuries—a severely dislocated shoulder and a piece of bone tearing away from my shoulder—were relatively minor when compared to what could have happened. But let's get back to the story…

After Joe and I gathered our wits, we analyzed the situation we were facing. Almost immediately my Air Force aviator survival training kicked in. I determined that Joe and I needed to come up with a plan of action—and we needed it fast. From the sun's low position on the horizon, I knew it would be getting very dark and very cold in short order. Joe and I had both suffered what we suspected were severe injuries. We were both in acute pain and much debilitated. Joe told me that every time he took a breath, fiery bolts of pain shot throughout his body. My shoulder racked me with some of the most intense pain I'd ever known, making focusing on anything, even a survival plan, much more difficult.

I am rarely without my GPS unit in the backcountry. On this particular day, however, I'd decided to leave it in camp because I knew our guide had his GPS in his daypack. Wrong choice. Lesson learned? Never…ever…leave camp or an unfamiliar backcountry area without a GPS! In my desire to lighten my daypack load, I'd broken one of my longtime, personal rules by choosing to rely on someone else for my safety and welfare.

With the sun getting lower by the minute, I knew we had to get back to camp for help. We looked at each other and quickly realized that neither of us knew the way back to camp. All I knew was that we needed to continue to the top of the ridge and turn left. After that I didn't have a clue. Neither did Joe. Due to our injuries, neither of us was in any shape to handle valleys and hills, so Joe and I decided that if we were to make it back to camp at all, assuming we could figure out where it was, we would have to keep to higher ground. This meant we would have to travel a much longer and more roundabout route. I quickly said a prayer and asked God to lead us home. I asked Him to help us place one foot in front of the other and guide us to camp.

Off Joe and I went…two banged-up hunters looking like something out of a bull-riding rodeo wreck hobbling up a game trail at a pace that would make a snail look like a racecar. With a useless arm dangling toward the ground like a broken wing and having to walk like Quasimodo to minimize the pain, there was no way I could carry my backpack and its internal water supply. Joe, fiery dinged-up ribs and all, volunteered to carry both our packs. Knowing that going into shock was a possibility for both of us, we stopped regularly for water and to check on each other for signs of shock or dehydration.

After what seemed like days but was really only hours, Joe and I came upon our missing guide. One of the other guides from camp was with him. They were riding toward us on the trail with our horses in tow. Two memories of this surreal scene remain vividly etched in my recollection. Not seeing anything resembling a look of remorse on the face of my horse, I really wanted to go over to him and give him a piece of my mind…or a bit more than that. Second, I recall looking up at the saddle on my horse and thinking, *No way!*

So in as cordial a way as I could think of, I informed the young guide leading the string that there was no possible way I could climb up on that horse with a busted-up arm. More so, with my recent rodeo-like experience fresh in my mind, there was no way I was going to climb back up on any horse in the foreseeable future. I recall thinking of the image of a boxing champ hovering over his fallen opponent with ominous words of warning echoing, "If you know what's good for you, you'll stay down!"

Believing my injuries were somewhat extensive and would require professional medical attention as soon as possible, and thinking that Joe might be in the same kind of shape or possibly even worse, I suggested the guide hightail it back to camp, use the cellular phone to call the Search and Rescue folks, and get a helicopter in the air. In response, the young guide with all of his 20-or-so years of wisdom informed me, "You've probably just got a dislocated shoulder. I think I can probably fix that!" The image of Mel Gibson's character from the 1980s film *Lethal Weapon* slamming his dislocated shoulder into a wall to repair it flashed through my mind. *Not in a thousand lifetimes, friend!* I thought. With all the willpower within me, I just thanked him for his offer and insisted on the helicopter.

Joe echoed my feelings about the horses, so once again he and I bowed our heads into the wind and stepped off on our trek up the mountain toward camp. Word of our misfortune had already gotten around by the time we reached camp. The cook had placed the call I'd requested to the outfitter's trailhead camp. Someone there placed a follow-up call to the county sheriff's office to initiate a rescue operation. I walked into camp on my own and quietly made my way to my tent. Totally spent, I tried to make myself as comfortable as possible. By now my entire body was shaking uncontrollably. Whether this was from the adrenaline, shock, the rapidly cooling outside temperature, or a combination of all three I don't know. I do remember that my biggest fear the entire time was not my injury but how I was going to break the news of this calamity to my new wife.

I am blessed with the most wonderful wife a man could ever ask for. She loves me with all her heart and encourages me daily to pursue my loves—elk hunting and writing. However, as a teenager, Rae Ann had lost her best friend in a horseback riding accident. And now, after only four months of marriage, this horse-related disaster happened to me. I had to find a way to let her know about the accident while assuring her I was in good hands and would recover. I sent a message to the outfitter to hold off calling Rae Ann until I was onboard the helicopter and in the hands of trained medical professionals, thinking that would minimize her fears. Not smart. Boy, did I have a lot to learn.

Time seemed to drag on forever as I lay in my tent alone, longingly anticipating the sound of the rescue helicopter. There was no position I could assume that relieved the nerve-racking pain. And now that the adrenaline had worn off, the agony was debilitating. I guess everyone got so caught up in preparing for the helicopter that they forgot they had two injured people in camp. When one of the other hunters finally came into the tent, I asked him if he would please check on me from time to time. From that moment on, one of my fellow hunters was always by my side.

I had been lying there for what I thought was an hour or so when one of the hunters, Spencer Ruff, whom I hadn't had much chance to get to know, walked in and asked how I was doing. Between the mind-numbing spasms of pain, I told him I was doing as well as possible given the circumstances, whereupon he came over and sat down on the end of my cot. He asked if he could pray for me. As a Christian, I am no stranger to prayer, having spent countless hours talking to the Lord for others. But this was new—having someone pray for me. Even now as I write this I am overcome with emotion as I relive that moment—remembering the generosity, sensitivity, and Christian brotherly love of my newfound friend. He bowed his head and prayed to the one God of heaven for me. Looking back, I believe Spencer's timely prayer made more difference in my recovery than all the medicine mankind could administer.

As the sun settled behind the purple mountains (yes, they really are purple when the sun is just right), I heard the most welcomed sound I'd experienced all week—helicopter rotors tearing through the cold, high-mountain air. I knew then that my ordeal was almost over and that I was going to survive. With hunter orange vests volunteered from every hunter and guide in camp outlining a makeshift emergency landing zone, a Flight-for-Life helicopter carrying angels of mercy clad in blue flight suits landed a few hundred yards from my tent. In no time, a flight nurse and medical technician were beside me, checking my vitals and preparing me for the quickest trip out of the mountains I've ever experienced.

As it turned out, I had a severely dislocated shoulder, which the emergency room docs were able to treat while I was out like a light—pain wimp that I am. Following my visit to the emergency room, I enjoyed the hospitality of the Holiday Inn in Grand Junction, Colorado, for the next two days while waiting for a mountain storm to pass so Rae Ann and a friend, a pilot, could fly to my rescue. I must have been a sight. I had two black eyes, cuts and bruises over 50 percent of my face, my arm was wrapped up, and I was wearing the same dirty, smelly, camo duds I'd had on since the accident. I must have been quite a spectacle in the hotel restaurant. I told folks who asked, and there were quite a few, that I'd gotten into a fight with a horse and lost.

YOUR FIELD NOTES

As a hunter, hunting consultant, and professional speaker, I've told this elk hunting story hundreds of times. It is a rare event when someone hearing it fails to offer a few words thanking me for taking the time to share the story and the lessons learned. To help you share your stories and start your own field notes, here are some questions to get you started. You can answer them here or, even better, get a small notebook and create your own official Hunter's Field Notes guide.

What events in the field shaped your life or made a significant impact on your life?

What insights or lessons did you gain from those events?

How might sharing those events and the wisdom learned make a difference in the lives of others?

A Continual State of Prayer

Every day we have opportunities to draw near to God the Father. Here's a thought: Why not remain in a continual state of prayer throughout the day? "That's not possible," you say. But it is. Prayer is more than words lifted up. It can also be a state of mind, a state of being where we *choose to remain in close proximity to God*, in close relationship to the One we love.

While I enjoy listening to Christian music, I am not very good with remembering the names of the artists. Recently, however, I was blown away by the lyrics of a song I heard on the radio. A few days later I heard it again, so I did an internet search for the title and learned the song was written by Bebo Norman and Jason Ingram. The title of the song is "Never Saw You Coming." A line in the chorus describes how I experience the state of continuous prayer. The words speak to the originality of experiencing God's total, unconditional love for the first time. It reflects having a very personal and amazing relationship with a best friend, with Jesus Christ. His love is all encompassing and absolutely fulfilling. It is perfect! It is also our model. When I consider how I need to love my wife, I look at how Christ loves me. While I can never match His love, I can use it to help me love Rae Ann more completely.

When I was a child, my brother and I were often babysat by my maternal grandmother. I curiously watched her walk around her small country house in western Tennessee singing and humming what I then called "church songs." As I was all of six or seven years old, I thought Nanny was a few cards short of a full deck, singing to the walls and such. It wasn't until I was in my late twenties and home visiting family that I asked her what her singin' and hummin' was all about. Her answer amazed me.

Nanny shared that in those days life was tough. There wasn't always enough money to go around, which caused her a great deal of sorrow and worry. Every day she would get up at three o'clock to prepare breakfast for my grandfather before he left for his job in a factory to make ends meet. After he would leave, her day began. In those days, few women worked outside of the home, so she took care of the house. Singing was how she remained in a continual state of prayer with the One she loved most in all the universe. This was how she coped with tough times. By singing those songs she was, in essence, praying...connecting to God. Wow, the power of prayer!

God gives every believer gifts. To some He gives more than one. My gifts are three: perceiver, teacher, and exhorter. As "perceiver," my intercessory prayer for you is that God will touch your heart today. I pray you will know how much He loves you and that He deeply cares and wants to be part of your daily life. The "teacher" in me says God created you for a purpose, a mission you are uniquely equipped to carry out. My "exhorter" side says to seek God with all your heart. Knock on His door, speak your heart to Him through prayer, and then listen for His answers. Answers will always come when you wait for them.

YOUR FIELD NOTES

What can you do to facilitate a continual state of prayer in your life?

Do you have a favorite Christian song that you can sing in your head?

If not the whole song, how about just a few words like "high and lifted up" or "holy, holy, holy"?

Do you have something small that will fit in your pocket that you can carry around with you that will remind you of your heavenly Father's love?

4

A View Through the Trees

Now we see things imperfectly...
but then we will see everything with perfect clarity

(1 Corinthians 13:12 nlt).

Just this morning as I was having a long-put-off quiet time with the One I love more than any other—the Lord of the universe—I joyfully found myself caught up in a spirit of awe and very personal worship that I hadn't experienced in some time. I had a music CD playing, and the sound reverberated around and through my body and soul. Before I knew it, my arms were stretched over my head, palms out, reaching for the God who loves me.

To fully understand where I'm coming from, you need to know I was raised in a very conservative Southern Baptist environment. Worship in church was, well, very, very regimented. Sunday morning services were strictly governed by the order of service with much emphasis on *order*. Dressed in their Sunday best, folks from the surrounding community would crowd through the doors with just minutes to spare as they hurriedly headed for "their" seats. Soon the choir director walked up to the pulpit, swinging his arms in an upward motion, asking all to rise as he led the faithful, who were all standing at attention, eyes straight forward, hymnals positioned appropriately to read from, through all four or five stanzas of however many songs it took to fill the allocated worship time in the service. I recall the words of some of those great old hymns that I still love, but for the life of me I can't recall one single instance in those days when the Spirit of God reached out to me through this time of worship. In all those years as a young boy in Sunday services, I don't recall ever getting even a brief glimpse of the God I was hearing so much about. As a normal, healthy, curious young person, I wondered why that was.

So much has changed in the past 40 or so years. I believe that had someone raised their hands in worship back in the "old" days at the church my family attended, people in church might have misinterpreted this act of personal worship and praise as some sort of seizure. They probably would have sought medical help as they quickly and quietly escorted the "suffering" person out of the sanctuary.

Well, here I am, many years later, and most times my worship in public is still somewhat inhibited by those old, conservative behaviors I learned so long ago. But often at those times my heart and soul cry out—even scream—to lift my hands to reach out to the One I love, to feel just a small touch of His Spirit. On this particular morning, when I'd finally fit in some quiet worship time, it was different. God the Creator had a plan! He knew how desperately I wanted and needed to be near Him. He knew how much He wanted me to know that He wanted to be near me—to comfort me and let me know that He was with me, that I was not alone.

So, as I said, the music flowed around and through me, and my inhibitions about spontaneous forms of worship melted away. It was just God and me, God and an audience of one. The untainted joy of being surrounded by His Holy Spirit was more than I could contain. My arms were over my head with my fingers spread open as I reached toward heaven. The more I stretched, the farther I wanted to reach. When I could stretch no more, God said, "That's far enough, My son. I am here." And He reached out and drew my spirit into His for a time. As I stood with tears flowing down my face and eyes closed, God prompted me to open my eyes and tilt my head upward.

At this time God had blessed my wife, Rae Ann, and me with a modest home that had a view that often took my breath away. Though we lived in a subdivision in a small town outside of St. Louis, our back deck was very private—even secluded—by a small forest that surrounded our backyard. I knew that just beyond this veil of forest leaves and branches there was another world—a world of noise, confusion, hurry, and stress, a world of pressure and challenges that often have no obvious solutions. But our back deck, with the forest that was just an arm's length beyond, was a retreat and a blessing. And on that wonderful day of worship, God was putting it to His good use.

You know, one cool thing about God is the way He communicates with His own when He really has something He wants us to get. I believe God gave us language to communicate with each other, but He reserved something else, something extraordinary and far more intimate for those times when He wants to communicate directly with us as individuals.

As He opened my eyes and turned my face toward Him, all I could see through the huge panes of glass between the forest and me were hundreds of irregular patches of blue sky breaking through the canopy of trees. They were like hundreds of small portals connecting my world to His. A view through the trees, so to speak.

As I tried to take it all in, it was just too much. I was overcome. I fell to my knees, my face to the floor, my palms still turned upward to Him. I must have been in that position for a minute or so when I felt His hands lift my face. To my astonishment, the view above had changed almost entirely. From my now-lower or more childlike position, the number of openings through the trees was considerably less. Where before there had been hundreds, now there were only a few. Straightaway God's words, as given to the apostle Paul for one of his letters to the Corinthians, came to mind: "Now we see things imperfectly...but then we will see everything with perfect clarity" (1 Corinthians 13:12 NLT). Actually a slightly altered version came to my mind: "Now *as children* we see things imperfectly...but then *as we grow to maturity in Him* we will see everything with perfect clarity." In my spirit I felt God saying, "Jay, this is the message I have for you. I want you to share it with as many people as you can. I want to show Myself to you and them. My heart is for you and them to know Me. I, God, desire a very personal and intimate relationship with you and all people. But because you humans can only handle so much of who I am, I will give you brief glimpses of Me from time to time. As a child, these glimpses will be fewer and smaller, but as you grow and mature, I will show you more."

=== YOUR FIELD NOTES ===

It's absolutely amazing what happens when we give God our undivided attention. Has God ever called your name? He called Lazarus by name, so why wouldn't He call you by name? Listen for it. Write down your thoughts as you consider the fact that if God desires a personal intimate relationship with each of us, why He wouldn't call us by our names.

Next time you and God are having some personal time, listen for your name. Write down your reaction.

Have you noticed that as your Christian faith has grown, God doesn't seem as "hands on" as He used to be in your life? Could it be that as your faith has matured, God knows you don't need as much hand holding as you did when your faith was less mature? This is a great time to share with others about how you came to your faith in Christ and how it has matured over the years.

When was the last time God showed you a bit of Himself? What was that like?

5

Just Between God and Me

Have you been journaling? Before you say "I'm a guy...and journaling or writing stuff down—that's not for me," hear me out. Let's take a look at men of history who have left us glimpses of their lives through their recorded prayers: King David, Winston Churchill, George Washington, Thomas Jefferson, General Robert E. Lee, General Ulysses S. Grant, General George S. Patton, John F. Kennedy, and George W. Bush, just to name a few. Putting your prayers to paper (prayer journaling) can be a powerful tool that helps you focus your prayer life by recording your petitions *and* God's responses. Over time, you'll be able to look back and see a visible record of how God has moved in your life. Each entry becomes a milestone in your life.

As a professional writer and Christian speaker, I am a witness to the fact that stories have the power to shape lives and futures by connecting the current generation with future generations. Prayer has the power to connect us with the God of the universe, thus allowing us to become part of "His story." One of the great tools good storytellers use to make a story memorable is to help their listeners (or readers) see their own connections to the story being told. I hope you are using my stories as jumping off points for putting your stories on paper (or computer) and even beginning to enjoy the process. You will continue to discover the value of creating a visible and lasting written record of your hunting adventures and your personal story. And now you can consider adding a new dimension—journaling your prayers.

How Does Prayer Journaling Work?

Hopefully you see the value of prayer journaling, so let's talk about how it works. Let me tell you another story that I believe will help.

I've always considered myself a guy's guy. I was an Eagle scout by 13, deer hunter by 14, an air traffic controller at 23, a military officer by 27, and a jet fighter pilot by the time I was 29. If ever there was a guy with testosterone overload it was me. Life was lived for experience and achievement. Little thought was given to prayer. For the first half of my life, my prayers consisted primarily of thanking God before meals (as I had been raised to do) and asking God to get me out of trouble (which happened all too frequently). Though I had accepted Jesus Christ as my personal Savior when I was 20, I figured I had purchased fire insurance so I could live life to the fullest on my own terms. To paraphrase one of my favorite comedians, Bill Engvall of the famed Blue Collar Comedy Tour, "I was just a guy."

At age 51, after two careers and one failed marriage of 28 years (it doesn't take a rocket scientist to see how that happened), God blessed me with the second greatest gift He could bestow—my absolute best friend and wonderful wife, Rae Ann. One of the attributes of second marriages is that, unlike first marriages where both partners' lives are usually a fairly clean slate, the spouses often bring a fair amount of baggage and practices into the relationship. Some bags are big and obvious, others not so much. One particular item that Rae Ann brought into our marriage came wrapped in a small binder that at first was usually kept out of sight. Not because it was a secret she was trying to keep from me, but more because it was deeply personal. It was her prayer journal.

As the early years of our new life together passed, I quietly observed Rae Ann's diligence as she pulled out her journal and jotted down a quick prayer for this person or that issue. Regularly, often more than once a day, she would return to her journal and place little stickers beside a particular entry. After a while my curiosity got the best of me.

"Honey, what's with the stickers?" I asked.

"That's easy," Rae Ann replied. "The stickers are *visible* reminders of God answering my prayers. By looking at all the stickers I am continually reminded of His faithfulness in my life and in the lives of those for whom I've prayed."

Wow! That is so cool, I thought. *Her prayer journal visibly reinforces how God demonstrates His love day after day.* "Okay," I said. "Then what about those that don't have stickers beside them?"

"Those are the ones where God said or is saying to me 'wait' or 'not now.'"

"What about the prayers where God just says no?" I asked.

"I mark those with a highlighter," she responded. "My prayer journal allows me to visually track God's hand in my life and the lives of those I pray for."

Didn't I just say that? Guys, we can do this too! A prayer journal can be a powerful tool for men. If you're like me, your life revolves around sticky notes (physical and digital) that are everywhere—my iPhone's calendar and notepad, Microsoft Outlook, my schedule, my to-do list. Why? Because there is just too much to keep track of. If I don't write it down, I forget it. Sound familiar? "Yeah, yeah, but I'm old," you say. "Too old to learn something new or develop a new habit." Or maybe you're saying, "Yeah, yeah, but I'm too young. I have too much to do to be taking the time to write stuff down." Trust me, this sort of memory management works for *all* ages. If we don't write it down, things that matter, that make a difference, can be lost or forgotten forever.

So here's how prayer journaling works. Getting started is pretty simple. Get a notebook. If you want a great-looking, leather-bound journal, that's fine. If you prefer an inexpensive, spiral-bound notepad, that works too. What's more important is that your prayer journal be readily available to you throughout your day…and possibly your night. It needs to be handy. You can never tell when you will want to jot down a note about a quick prayer or add a sticker or special mark when you see God's hand moving in response to a prayer. Have you ever had God wake you up in the middle of the night? I have. A bedside table is a great place to keep your journal.

Make sure to leave about an inch of space at the beginning of the first line of every entry. This is where you will track what happens with a sticker or note. I know. I can hear you. "Stickers? You've got to be kidding!" Actually, I'm not. Anything will do, but you can find almost any kind of small stickers at your local Walmart or grocery store. You can get a thousand smiley face stickers for a couple of bucks. Stash a few pages of these in the back of your journal. Consider them ammo. When God answers a particular prayer, place a sticker in the blank space at the beginning of the entry. As mentioned before, when God clearly says no, mark the entire entry with a highlighter.

Now you can track with just a glance God's ongoing work in response to your prayer life. Stickers mean a positive response. Highlighter means no or not yet. And an entry without a sticker or mark means God has yet to visibly act on that particular request.

Here is an important caveat: This process is not and never will be a test of God's responses to your petitions. Keeping score is not part of this exercise. Watching God's hand as He moves in and through your life as recorded in your journal reveals His active participation. Without this visible record, it can be difficult for your mind to keep track. We humans are visual creatures—especially men, so give prayer journaling a try.

Actively record every petition you offer up to God for a period of 90 days. At the end of that time, I suspect you will see one of two things: a very visible trail of God's hand moving throughout your life or nothing because you failed to accept my challenge and keep up with the journaling. Friend, this is entirely up to you. All I can do is encourage you. All too often we offer up our prayers and then move on with our lives with little thought to what happened. Do you want to see God's hand more visibly? Take up the 90-day challenge.

We Are Being Watched

Today two generations call me "Papa." I guess that means I'm getting old. I don't feel old...well, maybe a little when exercising one of my passions—hunting elk high in the Rockies. It seems like each year those peaks get a little higher and the valleys are a little deeper. But getting back to my point, there are at least two generations who are watching what I do and overhearing what I say. I willingly accept that as a huge responsibility. Notice I didn't say they *listen* to what I say. Though

I try to exhort some measure of wisdom into the lives of others, I've found that most folks learn more by how I live my life, by my *example,* more than how I *tell* them to live.

By tracking my prayers and the results, I can share parts of my journal or tell people about my journal, giving them an example to follow that also encourages them to be praying too. By journaling, you and I not only tell people God answers prayer and that praying is effective, but we can show visibly what we've experienced. I've witnessed lives changed, marriages healed, careers saved, challenging life situations reversed, and hearts altered as a result of the effective prayers of righteous men and women. What was the common denominator? A prayer warrior interceding for another. A prayer journal is a great way to document the power of prayer.

Let me share another story that demonstrates how truly powerful prayer is.

The Testimony of Prayer

Not too many years ago a friend of mine was undergoing one of the most difficult times of his life. He had inadvertently become mixed up in an activity that got the attention of law enforcement. As a result, he was arrested and charged with a crime that, if proven, had the potential to send him to prison. Because my friend had no past criminal history, the court granted his petition for bail after he'd spent a terrifying night in a county jail. Following that dreadful time, he spent a number of years awaiting the decision of the court. He said it was like living with a sword hanging over his head, never knowing if or when it might fall.

Throughout this time of waiting and going through the actual trial, family and friends gathered around him and prayed earnestly. One brother who was very close to him told my friend, "This is not your battle to fight. This battle is God's. You must remain faithful and know that God will have victory because you belong to Him."

My stunned friend asked, "How do you know this?"

"Because," the brother answered, "I have prayed about this. I took your situation before the God of all creation. I have petitioned our

Father in heaven, and this is the answer He gave to me to give to you. 'This is not your battle to fight!'"

Finally the day of truth arrived, and my friend was summoned to court to learn his fate. Now when he shares the entire story, people see that Satan clearly had his hand in this matter because for years my friend's days were filled with mostly fear and dread. The Bible tells us there is only one source of fear, and that is the enemy—Satan. In this case, the devil successfully used fear to distract my friend from what God wanted him to be doing with his life.

On this day of judgment, my friend was sitting alone outside the courtroom where, as he tells it, he heard a quiet but distinct voice. "The voice," he said, "was as clear as if the person speaking was sitting right beside me." Yet when he turned his head to look, no one was there. The entire hallway, which just moments before was crowded with people, was empty. Yet the voice had called him by name and said simply, "I am going to amaze you." That was all there was to it. Well almost. Immediately following those words, my friend described being overcome with peace. He described it as a warm, gentle wave washing over his body, bringing a peace unlike anything he had ever experienced. For that moment time seemed to stand still, and all other sounds were extinguished.

Minutes later the door to the courtroom opened, and he was called in. As he stood before the judge, many things were said, yet he heard only two wonderful words: "case dismissed." Two words and his ordeal was over. He was free. The charges had been dropped. He was free to return to the world. Free to return to his life and those he cared about and loved. Free to forever serve the God who had truly amazed him in his time of need. "The effective prayer of a righteous man can accomplish much" (James 5:16 NASB).

YOUR FIELD NOTES

Do you have a place where you can be alone for five minutes? Where is it? What makes it perfect for solitude?

Every morning, go there and ask God, "What do You want me to do today?" Write down some of His answers.

Do you have time in the mornings and afternoons on your drive to and from work to spend a few minutes listening to what God has to say to you? Keep this book or a notebook handy. Don't write while you're driving, but when you get to work or home, write down what God said.

What do you think God would say to you right now if you put this book down and said, "Here I am, God! What do You have for me today?" Write it down.

6

A Most Memorable Elk Hunt

My 2009 elk hunt preparation actually started after an unsuccessful archery elk hunt in 2007. Let me explain. First, does it not seem odd that whenever we do something noteworthy there is rarely anyone around to share the moment with? Yet when we fail, especially when big game hunting, there is often someone close by to witness the blunder? And these days that person usually has a recorder on hand... and possibly a contract to capture and publicize the sordid details of your hunt (in my case, anyway).

Such was the case in 2007. I was hunting with my good friend and first-class outfitter Bill Glisson, owner of "The Timbers at Chama," located in New Mexico. Our five-day elk hunt culminated in my missing what appeared to be an unbelievably easy 23-yard shot at a nice bull elk on the last day. (In my defense, I was attempting to thread an arrow through a small opening in thick brush while praying as hard as I could that God would steer that bull behind the opening.) As has happened so many times in my life, God did His part, and the bull did, in fact, walk broadside behind that miniscule opening.

=== **YOUR FIELD NOTES** ===

Have you ever had God answer your prayer...only to discover you weren't prepared to do your part? What was the situation?

Back to my 2007 elk hunt. My arrow managed to center punch a one-inch branch of gambel oak on the edge of the "window of opportunity." I was really hoping the guy with the video camera was napping or at least looking the other way, but no, of course not. A year later all of America watched yours truly on national TV miss what appears to be a slam-dunk. Some days we eat bear, and some days the bear eats us. Such is the life of a hunter.

After I turned to Bill and admitted missing the shot, he chuckled a little. Actually it was more than just a little. He said the folks all the way back at the ranch probably heard the sound of my arrow striking that tree. Then Bill blew me away. He went the extra mile and invited me to return to The Timbers the following year to try my luck again at closing the deal on a New Mexico bull. Needless to say I accepted! I started to plan my 2008 hunt before I even left the ranch.

God, however, had a more indirect path in mind.

YOUR FIELD NOTES

When was the last time you went the extra mile for a friend? What did you do and why?

How did it turn out?

When was the last time a friend or family member went the extra mile for you? What did that person do? Why do you think that person did it?

How did that act affect you?

God Can Use Anything for His Glory

In April of 2008, I went to our family doctor for an annual physical…after some not-so-gentle persuading from Rae Ann. She says she loves me too much to leave my health at risk. About a week after my visit, my doc's nurse calls and informs me that my PSA numbers—test scores for prostate cancer—were above what is considered normal for men of my age. She suggested I make an appointment with a specialist for a biopsy. No big deal.

I made the appointment, had the biopsy (not so much fun), and waited for the test results. A few days later, the urologist's office called and asked me to make an appointment to come in to talk with the doctor about the biopsy results. The nurse also suggested I bring my wife with me. I recall two sensations as I hung up the phone. First, I wasn't sure my heart was still beating. Second, I trembled as I thought, *They want me to bring Rae Ann. This can't be good.*

To get to the point, I was told I had early stage prostate cancer. I'm not sure of anything that was said immediately after I heard the word "cancer." Life suspended as a dense fog of apprehension settled over me.

━━━━━━━━ **YOUR FIELD NOTES** ━━━━━━━━

Have you experienced fear like this? If yes, what caused it and how did it affect you?

Did you share this with the people close to you? If yes, how did you do it?

What did you learn through the entire experience?

To whom did you turn to draw strength from?

Within weeks of learning I had cancer, I placed a call to my friend Bill in Chama and told him the news. I also shared that I wouldn't be able to go to New Mexico for the 2008 hunt due to the upcoming cancer treatment. Bill said that his concern was more for my well being, and that the hunting offer was good for as long as I needed it. What a true friend. (I hope you have at least one friend like Bill!)

As I came to grips with some of the most devastating news of my life, God actively revealed Himself in very personal and practical ways. He reminded me often of His promise to stand by me no matter what: "I will be with you; I will not fail you or forsake you" (Joshua 1:5 NASB).

First, Rae Ann took my hand and assured me that whatever was going to happen we would go down that road together. (We hold hands more than any two people I know.) She too would never leave me or forsake me. What a comfort in this time of stress, fear, and anxiety to know I had God and people who loved me to come alongside me in support. I was never going to be alone.

YOUR FIELD NOTES

Think about a time in your life when God gave you peace and comfort during a difficult time. What was the situation?

How did you know God was with you?

Were you sure He would hang in there with you no matter what? If yes, what gave you that confidence?

The second indicator was a peace like nothing I had ever experienced. It washed over and through my spirit. Hope replaced fear. Awe replaced anxiety. I was surrounded and filled with God's Holy Spirit.

Third, a clarity of purpose formed within me as God confirmed that everything that had happened in my life, including this cancer, was going to be put to use for His greater purposes. He essentially said, "Jay, do you remember that I promised to have a plan for your life? I do! You are going to make a difference in the lives of many. The stories of the trails we have traveled together, as well as this trail you are about to set out on, will encourage others and draw them closer to Me."

> "I know the plans I have for you," declares the LORD, "plans
> to prosper you and not to harm you, plans to give you hope

and a future. Then you will call on me and come and pray to me, and I will listen to you. You will seek me and find me when you seek me with all your heart. I will be found by you," declares the LORD (Jeremiah 29:11-14).

The good news was that the cancer in my body was detected at a very early stage. Prostate cancer identified early is one of the most treatable and survivable cancers. Knowing the prevalence of prostate cancer in men today and because her family had a history of cancer, Rae Ann regularly encouraged me to have a physical and all the ensuing tests. As a result, the PSA test initiated a series of other tests that identified the cancer and allowed it to be treated before it became life-threatening. My radiated "seed" implant therapy for prostate cancer, while not a walk in the park, was fairly simple and produced outstanding results.

Friend, this is my personal encouragement to you. Get the test done! Prostate cancer, if undetected and untreated, can end your life. Your family loves you, and they deserve more than the typical male arrogance or indifference when it comes to physical maladies. Get the test done!

In a little over 18 months after being diagnosed, I was cancer free and ready to take Bill up on his offer of a redo elk hunt. And God had even more blessings in store!

"Plans to Prosper You"

December 12, 2009. The first day of my New Mexico elk hunt began at four in the morning. Needless to say, when the alarm clock went off my body screamed, "Are you out of your mind?" But my hunter's heart said, "Get moving, bro! Let's do this." After a quick breakfast of steaming coffee, cold cereal, and fruit, we were off to hopefully slay a beast.

Outside temperatures that week ranged from a high of 20 degrees (yes, I said a *high* of 20 degrees) to almost 20 below zero. Mid-December in northern New Mexico can be bone dry in some years and covered in a blanket of heavy snow in others. In 2009, it was not bone dry. The snow depth varied from as little as 8 inches to more than 30 inches. On any given day a few years before, such conditions would have given me pause. However, this 55-plus hunter didn't pause. I had overcome the big "C," and I was not going to allow a little cold and snow to keep me from a hunt I had anticipated for almost two years!

Every morning Bill, my friend and hunting outfitter; Gator, a hunting guide in training; John "Shooter" MacGillivray, a videographer; and I loaded up in Bill's big red pickup and headed to a nearby ranch Bill leased.

For those uninitiated to elk hunting, it is predominantly a "spot and stalk" process. Hours upon hours are spent glassing long distances with binoculars and spotting scopes in the hopes of spying a nice "shooter" bull or cow (an elk that meets the legal requirements for the hunt and is within weapon range). In our case, on this particular hunt, we spent many freezing hours and walked what seemed like a hundred miles as we made our way from vantage point to vantage point looking for shooter bulls. For three days all we got for our efforts were long-range views of cow elk—hundreds of them, in fact. But, alas, no bulls. After three days of this, Bill scratched his head and wondered if we were ever going to hook up with our prey. According to Bill, in most years at this time the mature bulls have recovered their energy that was burned off during the craziness of rut and would be together in bachelor groups feeding on what grass they could find. This year the bulls were nowhere to be found.

Day four went the same way.

I have to admit by day five I was just about worn out, as were the other members of our camouflaged band. The subzero temps and deep snow had taken a lot more out of us than we wanted to admit. That last morning wake-up call was the toughest of them all for me. But hope burned inside that today would be special. I just didn't know how special it would actually be.

It was mid-morning, and we had been slogging our way through some fairly deep snow as we wound through a small stand of juniper brush. Bill was in the lead, with me close on his heels. Gator and John, with his video camera, were bringing up the rear. (John is really a trooper. His gear was professional quality and heavy. The camera alone weighed in around 20 pounds and was probably worth $80,000 or so. Then there was the tripod that probably weighed nearly as much, plus all of his cold weather gear. Yet John never complained, and he was never more than a few steps behind me so he could capture any exciting moments or interesting shots. What a guy!)

As we neared the far edge of the junipers, Bill's right fist came up in the traditional signal to stop and hold tight. Bill turned to me and indicated he wanted me to come forward quietly. He had noticed a single antler rising above a small rise in the snow about 100 yards in front of us. I pulled out my binoculars. As I glassed, I saw another set of antlers. There were two spike bulls, probably lying in the snow sunning themselves. From this vantage point, all we could see were the antler tips.

As I continued to glass the meadow, I caught a faint movement on the far side. Standing broadside was one of the most beautiful bulls I've ever seen. He was positioned against a backdrop of dark pines. His tawny hide looked almost golden in the sunlight and was a stunning contrast to his mane that was nearly black. The juxtaposition against the snow and trees was spectacular. His antlers, while not huge, were more than respectable and perfectly symmetrical. It was like a postcard.

My heart rate went up a little. I pointed him out to Bill, and he quickly handed me a set of shooting sticks that would provide a good gun rest if I elected to take a shot while standing. Considering that we were in more than two feet of snow, I really didn't have much of a choice. I placed my rangefinder on top of the sticks and calculated the bull was a whopping 474 yards away. *Whoa! That's a far poke in anyone's book,* I thought.

I wanted this bull big time! We had hunted hard, and this was the last day. I had a decision to make. I knew my Remington .300 Ultra Mag was up to the task, but was I? Well, there was no time like the present to find out. I saddled up my rifle on the shooting sticks and cranked my 4-12X variable scope all the way up to the stops. I got comfortable and worked to get my breathing under control—no easy task at this point. Three separate times I went through my process of preparing for the shot. Each time I came up with the same answer—the shot was too far for me to take ethically. I was just not sure I could make the shot for a clean kill. Cold, tiredness, crosswind, and distance all came together at that critical moment. I made the only call I could. I told Bill I wasn't sure I could deliver a good, fatal shot and was going to have to pass on the opportunity.

I knew I made the right decision, and the others agreed, but for the next several hours I relived that moment over and over, wondering if there was something I could have done differently that would have changed the outcome. I must have apologized a dozen times to Bill and John. Finally they told me to just let it go.

YOUR FIELD NOTES

Have you found yourself in a similar life situation? Where one part of you said, "Go for it!" and another part said, "Wait! Not so fast!"? What was the situation? How did it work out?

How did you make your decision?

What lessons did you learn?

We hunted hard the rest of the day. As the sun descended toward the tops of the western slopes, I felt my heart sinking lower and lower. The day and the hunt were drawing to a close. We were glassing a nice muley buck as he fed in a sage flat while a herd of around 200 cow elk (not a single shooter bull in the bunch!) grazed a few hundred yards in front of us.

I stood there, taking in this beautiful scene, when a nagging feeling came over me. I decided I was not going to end this day looking at elk I couldn't take. I suggested to Bill that we head back toward the mountain where we'd encountered the golden bull earlier. I knew it was a long shot, but it was better than no shot in my mind. Bill agreed, so we grabbed our gear and headed in the opposite direction from the largest group of elk we had seen all week.

On the mountain, Bill was up front as usual. We had only traveled a few hundred yards when something got his attention. He instantly brought his binoculars to his eyes and, almost as quickly, turned to me and said, "Jay, you're not going to believe this, but that bull from this morning just came down off that mountain and is in a sage flat about a quarter of a mile in front of us!" With the sun getting closer to the horizon by the second, we looked at our watches knowing that the end of legal shooting hours, as well as the hunting season, was getting very close. He asked, "Are you up for a run in the snow?" Without thinking for a second I said, "Yes!" Off we went—a band of hunter brothers loaded down with gear, bone tired, and very cold. Remember, at the time I was 55 and had recently recovered from cancer treatment. I'm sure it was the Holy Spirit who filled me with stamina and gave me the strength and courage to make the quarter-mile sprint through deep snow. What an awesome God we have!

"Plans to Give You Hope and a Future"

I recall thinking about halfway to the best shooting vantage point that by all measures I should have keeled over from exhaustion. Yet here I was, running in deep snow like a twentysomething man in his prime. We ran, keeping a stand of juniper trees between us and the bull. Finally we came to a stop on the edge of the junipers and slowly picked our way through, hoping for a glimpse of the bull on the other side without getting busted. Bill's right fist came up quickly, followed by a crook of his index finger inviting me to go up to where he was.

Bill said, "Jay, the bull is right over there." He pointed.

Now this is where it gets really comical. All week I'd been having a problem with my glasses fogging up when I looked through my binoculars or scope. The extreme cold air combined with my warm breath was continually fogging up the glass. Bill had watched me battle with the fog until he couldn't stand it anymore. He asked if I really needed the glasses. I said I'd go without them and see how it went. My vision isn't really bad, so I'd started keeping my glasses in my inside shirt pocket—under three layers of clothing.

So now I'm standing beside Bill, and he is telling me that the bull is about 250 yards in front of us. I'm looking but I'm just seeing a lot of fuzzy open space beyond the first 100 yards. It was a laugh or cry situation. I chuckled to myself when I realized I might have to explain how I had to pass on the same bull again, this time because of a seemingly insignificant decision to not have my glasses easily accessible. Suddenly the solution came to me.

"Bill, give me the shooting sticks!" I whispered. I saddled up my rifle in the general direction of the bull, brought my scope to my eye, and there as clear as day was that beautiful golden elk! I had placed my faith in God that He would bring this hunt to His ordained conclusion, and that when He did I would be better prepared than I had been back in 2007. And here was His answer! I quietly thanked Him for the opportunity as I lightly touched the trigger. The report of the .300 Remington Ultra Mag had barely faded when that golden bull fell after taking a few short steps. I looked at my watch. There were eight minutes of legal day left.

God is faithful to finish the work that He begins. In this case, the hunt of a lifetime ended with Bill and me kneeling by my bull and exclaiming our thanks for the success God had delivered!

YOUR FIELD NOTES

Have you experienced a similar situation? Perhaps a hunt where everything you'd hoped for seemed to come together? Where were you? What was the situation?

How did that make you feel? Did you do anything special to celebrate?

Did you get to share that moment with someone? If yes, who? And what was that person's reaction?

7

Talking with God

Did you notice that on that elk hunt in Chama I connected with God more than once during the course of my time there? If you're used to praying with your head bowed and your eyes closed, my casual conversation with God may have seemed a bit off the reservation to you. As a child, I was taught to pray the same way most were. Head down, hands together before me, eyes closed. I'm not in any way taking issue with having a reverent posture for prayer. But if you are a more formal prayer person, I'd like to introduce you to the joys and blessings of "conversational prayer."

As my personal relationship with God, my loving heavenly Father, has matured over the years, the form and content of my prayer life changed as well. There are still times when I close my eyes and reverently submit to Him in a spirit of supplication and adoration. There are times when I stand or sit alone in the center of an empty room with my hands stretched heavenward, my body echoing my desire to reach out and join my spirit with His.

My favorite times with the Lord, however, are when I just talk to Him. And those times seem to happen more and more frequently. Out of nowhere, I just start a conversation with Him. Whether sitting at my desk, driving down the road in my Expedition, or just lying in bed before I drift off to sleep I enjoy some personal communion time with Jesus. I enjoy these conversations.

Not too long ago I even used this conversational prayer format in a small group environment at church. Granted, as it was a new concept to some, it took a few minutes for the people to feel at ease, but once they got started, conversational prayer flowed freely. One after another, folks just starting talking to God as if He were physically right there in the room, an active part of our small group. And He was, of course!

Conversational prayer has no predetermined structure. It is what I call "free form." By that I mean there is no particular order or form. It is a conversation. It is sharing your thoughts, your concerns, your hurts, your joys openly and without any hindrance or constraint. It's similar to any other conversation you engage in. There is no requirement to hit certain points, no required language or terminology, no specific order. So what does conversational prayer look like? Here's an example:

> God, what a great day this is. It's raining out and to be honest, I'm getting a little tired of the rain. But just the other day I was talking with a buddy in San Antonio who told me that they are on water rationing and only allowed a couple thousand gallons per week for their entire household and property. I'm so thankful for the rain.

> Lord, I'm starting to get settled in our new home here in Versailles. It is quite a change from our previous home near St Louis. The noises are different. Actually, since we live in town, there are a lot of noises, but I'm starting to get used to it. The people are different. They are so friendly. You know what, God? I love it. Eight years ago You heard me tell Rae Ann that I would *never* move to Kentucky. Colorado was my home forever and ever. Well, as You know, this most recent move was my idea.

> I can't believe how much my heart and life have changed over these past 10 years. Thank You, God, for Your faithful friendship and gentle guiding hand. Thanks for caring and providing for our family and for bringing us safely through some very difficult times. Thank You for our new granddaughter, Kyndal!

> I've never experienced such complete, unconditional love before. For years I didn't realize You could be my best

friend, someone I can talk to anywhere, anytime, for any reason. Thanks, Lord. I really love You.

And by writing out that conversation, I just had quality time with God while writing a book! Give conversational prayer a try. Our God hears everything. Your prayer, your conversation with Him, is an integral part of the relationship He so desires to have with you.

Whoa! Did you notice that "R" word: "relationship"? Where does that fit into a hunter's legacy? I'm glad you asked. We'll take a look at it in the next chapter.

YOUR FIELD NOTES

Have you ever had a conversation with God? Give it a try. Yeah, right now! Okay, what was it like?

Make conversations with God part of your family time. Even prayer at mealtimes could become a family conversation with God about the day's events. Why not try it out this week. Write down how you will implement this suggestion this week. How did it go?

8

It's Always Been About Relationship

I can't tell you how many times in my Christian life I've heard the words "have a personal relationship with Jesus Christ." I also can't count how many times those words rang hollow for me when I was younger. More recently, my wife was telling me about this well-meaning Christian lady whose first words in the world to Rae Ann were, "Let's get something out of the way right off the bat, honey. Do you know Jesus Christ as your personal Savior?" Now, neither my wife nor I were put off by what was surely said with good intention, but the way it was said and the context in which the question was asked didn't strike home as this lady probably intended.

If you have played baseball or golf, you know that perfect sound that a good solid hit makes when a baseball impacts the sweet spot of a bat or the same of a well hit drive off the tee. If you are a hunter, you know the sound that a well-placed bullet or arrow makes when it impacts the buck or bull. It rings true and solid. It's unmistakable and we know the outcome even before we see it. The sound communicates to all within hearing an effort well done. I believe that herein may lie the difference between a true, life-altering, personal relationship with God and the fire insurance faith I had when I was young. A true relationship results in the desire to share God's great gift of salvation with everyone in a way that reflects His love, His mercy, and His grace.

A zillion years ago, as in "in the beginning," man (you and me) was created by and in the image of God (Genesis 1:26-27 NASB). The apostle Paul states that as believers we were predestined to become "conformed to the image of His Son" (Romans 8:29 NASB). Okay, let's take that a step further. If by God's design we are destined to be conformed to the image of His Son, would it not stand to reason that it implies God desires a relationship with us? Father and Son—and man made in the Son's image.

Now take a look at the significant and loving relationships present in your life: spouse, children, brothers, sisters, parents, and friends. For any of those relationships to thrive and grow, participants must be willing to make the effort to sustain the relationship—and then follow through. Doesn't that sound reasonable? My life experience confirms this. Additionally, in relationships, the ratio of what we usually get out of them is close to what we put into them. That's not rocket science. An effort well done on both parts generally produces a strong and mutually rewarding relationship. If our effort is less, why should we be surprised to find ourselves in a relationship that isn't what we expected it to be?

Speaking of effort, how much we put into and get out of relationships depends not only on how much energy we expend but also in how we go about it. Let me explain.

Elk Hunting Basics

I moved to Colorado and began elk hunting in the Rockies during the 1980s. As I didn't know the first thing about elk hunting, elk habitat, or hunting in the mountains, it probably won't surprise you that I went four long years before I ever laid eyes on a live elk in the wild. Did I make the effort? Absolutely! I went as far as I could get from anything resembling civilization, parked my truck, put on my camo gear, grabbed my bow or rifle, walked up the nearest mountain, sat down near a game trail, and waited patiently for the elk to come by. Season after season I waited.

Are you thinking I must not be the brightest bulb in the pack? If you have experience in high-country elk hunting, you may need to get up off the floor and stop laughing so hard at my ignorance in those days. You don't want to have a physiological incident and embarrass yourself. Did I make an effort? Yes. Was my effort an effort well done? Not hardly.

Actually, I am a fairly smart guy. This waiting strategy had worked successfully for me when hunting whitetail deer, so I figured it would work for elk too. I grew up deer and turkey hunting in western Tennessee and Arkansas. Hunts with my dad and brother usually consisted of getting up at the reasonable hour of six in the morning, driving an hour or so to public land, and then walking around all day or sitting on game trails looking for something to shoot with our bows. Covered with camouflage greasepaint, we were a sight in those days. We killed a few deer and even a few turkeys, but mostly we walked and sat. Oh, and my dad smoked like a steam engine even in the woods. (He was never far away from a pack of Kools.) Needless to say, I hadn't picked up the skills and essentials of elk hunting, such as scent management, understanding and knowing the wind, range estimation techniques, equipment knowledge, and "spot and stalk" hunting.

I've learned that elk hunting ain't deer hunting. (And yes, I've become successful at filling my elk tags. You can read more about my adventures in my books *Elk Hunting 101, Elk Hunting 201, Elk Hunting 301,* and *Answers for Elk Hunters.* For more information, go to my website www.elkcamp.com.)

YOUR FIELD NOTES

Have you ever assumed you knew what you were doing while hunting or fishing only to discover you didn't know as much as you thought you did? Describe the situation.

What did you learn from that experience?

Have you implemented any strategies to head off being in a situation where you didn't know enough? What are they?

Since God created all that exists, and since He created man to be conformed to the image of His Son, and since Jesus willingly laid down His life for us, I think we can safely assume that God's level of effort in our relationship is to the max. So what can we do to deepen our relationship with Him?

The quality of our effort as it applies to our relationship with God depends on the answer to these questions: How important is it to us to know God on a personal level? In other words, what kind of priority are we willing to give to drawing closer to our Lord and Savior? Going beyond mere philosophical or academic interest, what value do we give to knowing and being known by God? What are we willing to do to ensure that we are in a deep, meaningful relationship with God? How badly do we want a close relationship with God? What is our commitment level?

Daring to Commit

In what I refer to as "my previous life," especially the days of my youth, I was in the United States Air Force. I was a weapons system officer flying F-4 Phantom jets all over the world. On occasion, I was selected to attend air shows where we would do flybys and then park the jets and stand around looking cool while talking to the crowd and answering questions. Growing up, I never had the opportunity to talk to a real fighter pilot, so I figured and hoped that the time spent talking to people at the shows was a positive influence in their lives. Because I enjoyed it so much, I did a lot of shows and talked with hundreds of people about flying and the air force.

At almost every show I was asked the same question: "What do I need to do to become a fighter pilot?" My answer was always the same.

I told them they have to determine how badly they wanted to be one. They have to be willing to sacrifice to be successful. They have to be willing to place their goal high on their priority list, letting some other things fall away. That is the level of effort you have to make to become a fighter pilot. This achievement is not as much about education or eye/hand coordination as it is about the energy a person is willing to expend to make it happen. Very few good fighter pilots I knew were academic overachievers, but all were focused, committed, and disciplined.

============================ **YOUR FIELD NOTES** ============================

So, when it comes to God, how badly do you want a close, personal relationship?

What are you willing to do? What level of commitment are you prepared to commit to so your relationship with Him will thrive and grow?

Here is the greatest part of this story, my friend. When God looks into your heart and sees your high level of desire to commit to a relationship with Him, He does all the heavy lifting. Essentially you just have to walk through the door. He says come, follow Me, and I will carry your burdens (Matthew 11:28-30).

============================ **YOUR FIELD NOTES** ============================

Do you want to have a personal relationship with God? He loves you! His Son, Jesus, died so you can have an intimate connection with God now and forever. To start on this exciting adventure, you only have to invite Jesus into your heart and life. You can pray this prayer or something similar:

> God, I just can't do this all myself. I need Your help. I want to be part of Your life. I want You to be part of mine. I know that Jesus was Your Son. I acknowledge His death for my redemption. I want You to be Lord of my life. Amen.

Do you already know Jesus personally? If yes, describe how you came to know Him.

What can you do to help your relationship with Jesus be healthy, vibrant, and growing?

Look at your previous answer and put a check mark by the ones you will follow through on. Then include time to accomplish your first choice in your regular schedule.

9

The Trail Less Traveled

Some years ago I went through some of the most difficult days of my life. In a matter of months I lost my marriage, my home, and my job. My future looked bleak and uncertain. With so many failures, so many sources of devastation hitting me all at once, I felt lost and very much alone.

One afternoon I was at home pondering this state of affairs. Like so many others in desolate situations, I found myself on my knees crying out to God. Not just crying, but wailing, with tears like a river running down my face. I recall my arms were stretched heavenward though this was not by my design—it just happened, as if it were a natural posture. This was not a mere cry to God asking Him to please help me get out of this painful place in my life like I had done so many times before. I was far beyond that! I felt total and utter hopelessness. I couldn't see a future for me, and I was unsure that my life had ever had any meaning or purpose. I had come to that place that men of letters call "the end of one's self."

At some point my tear ducts ran dry. I was just standing in the middle of a room in my home with my arms and face lifted heavenward. That is when God reached out and gave me a vision that is as real today as it was back then. In my vision I was standing between two roads. The road on the right was huge. It was a multilane highway that was straight and went for miles and miles. I could see everything on the road from start to finish. The other road on the left was a small dirt one, almost a trail. The center of the road was overgrown with grass, and there were ruts everywhere. The dirt road went a short distance and then made a hard turn to the left and disappeared into the woods. There was nothing on either side of the trail—no road signs, buildings, or anything.

I looked back over my shoulder and saw the point where the roads that were now two had once been one. I looked down and realized I was standing in the center of the large road. As I pondered this scene, it became clear to me that I was on the wrong road. As soon as I thought, "Do I need to go back and start over?" my vision changed. An arching wooden bridge formed, spanning the distance between the two roads. Standing in the center of the bridge was Jesus. He said, "Jay, you do not have to go back. Follow Me."

Jesus put out His hand. I reached out. Taking His hand, we walked across the bridge—away from the wide and long road that seemed to go straight to nowhere forever and headed toward the dusty trail that turned left and was soon out of sight. As Jesus and I stepped off the bridge onto the dusty road together, I took one last look back at the road I had traveled most of my life. The big road and all that it represented faded away, as did the bridge. Jesus Christ and I were alone on what I have come to call "the trail less traveled" (with a nod to Robert Frost).

I walked with Jesus down this new road into a new life on the trail less traveled. Today I still walk that overgrown, dusty road. It is the road of faith. Jesus is my guide, and my decision to take His hand and cross the bridge with Him has made all the difference in my world.

I don't know how long I'd been just standing in the room, but shapes and sounds came back into focus. I realized I was back. I knew something within me had changed forever. Something wonderful and miraculous had happened! For the first time in my life, I understood what hope means. The darkness of despair had been chased away. The emptiness of being alone was replaced by joy. Joy at being alive. Joy at knowing I had a future. Joy that I had come to the end of me and was now in a full-time loving relationship with my best friend, Jesus, a carpenter from a little town called Nazareth.

"I know the plans I have for you," declares the LORD, "plans to prosper you and not to harm you, plans to give you hope and a future. Then you will call on me and come and pray to me, and I will listen to you. You will seek me and find me when you seek me with all your heart. I will be found by you," declares the LORD, "and will bring you back from captivity. I will gather you from all the nations and places where I have banished you," declares the LORD, "and will bring you back to the place from which I carried you into exile" (Jeremiah 29:11-14).

YOUR FIELD NOTES

Have you experienced despair? What was the situation?

What alleviated or helped alleviate the situation?

Has God ever given you a vision for your life? If yes, describe where you were and how the vision came to you.

Describe the vision.

How did the vision impact or change your life?

10

Hunting Buddies

Not too many years ago, Roger and I decided we were going to host an elk camp in Colorado. We wanted to go beyond the ordinary and do something almost unheard of in the elk hunting community. So we invited a few good friends but also opened the camp up to anyone God brought our way.

If you're familiar with elk camps, you know that inviting strangers is almost unheard of among veteran elk hunters. Elk camp is considered by many to be holy ground—a place where only a select few who have *earned* their place are entitled to enter. That's why our idea to welcome anyone who came was quite out of the norm.

All told, we ended up with 19 people in camp that year. Talk about a crowd! I guess that almost half of the guys in camp didn't know the other half when we all gathered. But elk camp is a magical place where worldly trappings are left behind and friendships are born or rekindled. As camps go, other than the challenge of feeding 19 hunters at one time in a 12 x 16 wall tent and the one hunter whose rock concert sound level snoring kept critters away at night, our camp time was enjoyable but not necessarily memorable.

There was one thing notable though. I rode home with a guy named Steve Chapman. He was a hunter who was fast becoming a good friend. A friend of mine introduced me to "Chapman," as he is known, when Steve and Annie were attending and performing at the twenty-fifth anniversary of Focus on the Family held in Colorado Springs. (Steve and his wife are award-winning musicians who travel North America sharing Jesus and promoting Christian family values.) Because Steve and I are both die-hard hunters, it didn't take long for this subject to find its way into our conversation. During the next year or so, we talked on the phone a few times and our paths crossed in various cities. Steve told me how he'd been bitten by the elk hunting bug on a previous trip to Wyoming. I invited him to come along on the elk hunting trip. I told him he could bring along family members or a friend because that was the general theme of this unique hunt Roger and I were planning. He accepted.

At the end of camp, it worked out that Steve and I were partnered for the five-hour drive back to Colorado Springs. Five hours is a long time to share with someone you don't know very well. Thankfully, our mutual love for the Lord, our families, and hunting made the time pass easier. And we both enjoyed the challenges of our respective writing careers. What I had worried might be a rather long and awkward drive home turned out to be a solid foundation for a growing friendship.

What point am I making? We never know when God will bring people across our paths who will have major impacts on our lives. While it had always been our rule to restrict our hunting camps to close friends who had "earned their bones," so to speak, God clearly had other plans this time around. Steve and I have become good friends, and he generously agreed to write the foreword to this book. Of course, I had to promise not to tell the world about the time he shot a cow elk at the bottom of a very deep geographical depression and the ensuing problems...

Hunting camp and the relationships that often grow out of these times together create memories that fuel our lives for years. When I decided to write this book, I knew my hunting camp buddies would be a large influence in the process and content. In my experience, the camaraderie that comes from hunting camps is a huge part of the overall experience of spending time in God's wonderful outdoors. Whether through tales told around a blazing campfire, quiet times shared with a buddy while watching a remote waterhole at midday, or maybe even times shared in a rig on the way to or from camp, strong relationships are forged. This brings to mind a tale of another true huntin' buddy.

Angus "Rex" Butler was the truest of friends and closest of brothers. Good friends are hard to find, and good huntin' buddies are even tougher to come by. In the 40-plus years I've been hunting, I've had the pleasure of being in the field with dozens, perhaps even hundreds of men of like mind when it comes to the pursuit of game for food, but I have known only a few I would call true huntin' buddies. These are men in whom I have placed absolute trust—even to the point of trusting them with my life year after year.

Rex and I had been occasional friends at the church our families attended in Monument, Colorado. Then we discovered our mutual love for elk hunting and wild things. When I reflect on what most impressed me about this huntin' buddy, it was that he was chronologically old enough to be my dad and then some, and also he was more than willing to be my mentor. Despite his age, during our trips afield over the years he had the stamina, drive, enthusiasm, and energy to be out of his bedroll frying bacon and scrambling eggs with enough Tabasco and onions to choke a horse. He'd have everything ready when my alarm went off and it was still darker than midnight and colder than the dickens. Although he had two bad knees, Rex walked me into the ground nearly every day during elk season. What passion he had! What love for the hunt! And he truly loved God and His creation.

In our years of crossing ice-crusted streams, climbing from basin to high-mountain bowls, and climbing to mountain peaks and back down, Rex helped mold my character. By his example he taught me patience and perseverance—qualities that have proven essential to successful hunts and to living a more fulfilling and Christ-centered life. Unless Rex got to talking about his wife, Lynn, he was a man of few words but his living example of Christ-likeness spoke volumes.

Elk hunting is hard work. Anyone who says otherwise has either never been or has never really tried. But chasing elk offers rewards far beyond the delicious backstraps on the table to those who are willing to brave an unsure talus slope or scramble over the next ridge. Huntin' buddy Rex was the one who first showed me what waited for me on the other side of the pain a person feels when only halfway up the mountain.

Have you hiked a few miles in the Rocky Mountains? It sure isn't flat! Going downhill isn't that memorable physically, but those mind-numbing uphill climbs that set thighs on fire and cause lungs to feel like exploding are engraved forever in a climber's remembrance. Rex helped me discover that climbing may hurt some, but it's only for a short while. On the other side of the discomfort exists a cooling rivulet of clarity of mind and spirit that many don't know exists. Had Rex not been willing to press on those extra miles and encourage me to come alongside him when I wanted to quit, I would never have learned what lies beyond the next ridge. I wouldn't be the successful elk hunter I am today. I wouldn't have found out that it's perseverance toward a goal that may seem out of reach that builds solid, honorable character. I may never have learned what it means to truly love my wife more than life itself.

Thank you, Rex! You made a grand difference in my life. I thank God for you and the times we shared in the high country. As friends and huntin' buddies go, you're a keeper.

Rex had his homecoming some years ago. He went to be with his Lord just a few short years after our last hunt together. As I pause and remember the times we shared in camp and the last days in his home, I'm filled to overflowing with love and friendship for this man who saw value in me and took me under his wing. I'm looking forward to seeing Rex when my days are through. Then we can go looking for wild things again.

YOUR FIELD NOTES

Do you have a close friend—someone who qualifies as a "huntin' buddy"? Where did you meet? How was your friendship forged?

What does your buddy add to your life? What do you add to his?

11

10 Great Tips

One of my purposes for writing this book is to encourage you to dig a little deeper and travel further along on your life trail. The following tips have encouraged me, motivated me, challenged me, and changed me. I hope you will take the time to consider and perhaps meditate on each one. You might want to write each one down on paper and carry it around for a week. Then each time you pull it out, think about the tip and ask God to reveal wisdom, truth, and insights on the subject. Don't forget to enter His input and your thoughts in your Field Notes journal.

- When you make the focus of your efforts giving God the glory, He will amaze you.

- Jesus gave His life for you; God sacrificed His Son for you.

- Like life, hunting is not as much about the end of the road as it is about the journey.

- The more you share, the more you give, the more breathtaking the journey.

- Purpose to make a positive difference in the life of someone every day.

- On a human level, nothing is of greater value than loving and being loved—especially when it involves a spouse.

- You will eventually find what you seek. What are you looking for?

- The greater the sacrifice, the more unbelievable the joy!
- You are never alone. Jesus is standing right beside you right now.
- Everything in this book was written and designed for a hunter—for you!

YOUR FIELD NOTES

What tips would you like to share with the people you love?

Two Trails Coming Together

One of the most valuable lessons I've learned in life is that there is almost always more than one trail that will take us to our desired destination. This fall I hope to pursue a huge muley buck in Colorado. Given the state of the economy, I've done a fair amount of shopping around to find the most economical way to travel from Kentucky to Colorado. The cost of flying was just about the same as it was to drive! The flight would total six hours or so, including layovers. Driving would take approximately 18 hours. By taking my own vehicle, I would have a lot more flexibility in my travel plans, but 18 hours is a long time to sit and drive alone across the country. Both methods of travel get me to the same place. Two trails, one destination.

Now that you've traveled along my trail, you have the great opportunity to travel with Roger on his. Roger and I began our journeys in different places and traveled many different trails over the years, yet by God's grace He brought us together, in part to encourage you on your journey.

Part 2

Roger's Trail

Introduction
by Roger Medley

Having access to private land in whitetail country is truly a blessing. This is exactly what I had while I was a bi-vocational pastor living in Virginia. The land was a prime spot for many reasons. The owner kept horses on the property, so the grass was rich and lush. It was surrounded by pine and oak trees. And best of all, it was on the way home from the office! All I had to do was park my truck, change my clothes, grab my bow or rifle, walk 50 yards to a ladder stand, and I was ready to go.

During this time I was introduced to an author named Steve Chapman. My wife had bought me a book called *A Look at Life from a Deer Stand*. I was spellbound by the way Steve could write. He is a songwriter and has a real gift for being able to place a person right in the middle of the story he's telling. He is also a guitar player and singer. I am too, so I could relate to this guy on many levels.

As I read his book, one of the things that really stuck out was the things the Lord was teaching him while he was in the field hunting. I actually became a little jealous! I wanted to hear from the Lord while hunting. At this time in my life, I was pastoring, but I'd hit a dry spell in my relationship with Christ. I was busy in my job, which included leading worship, song selection, handling the worship band rehearsal, leading worship on Sundays, preparing a message for Wednesday nights, teaching that message, and following up with first-time visitors.

Then the routine would begin all over again the next week. Sort of a "rinse and repeat" process that showed me that it was painfully clear I needed and longed for a freshness in my walk with Christ. I was in an arid land and hurting.

My walk with Christ needed a boost, and so did my passion for hunting. Usually two of the most exciting things about hunting are "Will I see something?" and "If I do, will I be able to take it?" In states that are overpopulated with wildlife, the authorities address the issue by giving hunters opportunities to harvest multiple deer. This was certainly the case in Virginia at that time. A "big game" license covered three deer, one bear, and two turkeys. So early in deer season there was little worry about being able to take what I saw. With all those options in the license, a hunter could take whatever came his way.

I should note one thing about the private property I was hunting on. It was the only piece of ground that deer could graze within several miles. The surrounding cover was too dense to support the growth of enough nutritional food. With multiple tags and hunting the only piece of grazing ground around, there was no question about seeing deer. Access to this land meant a short season. Some people think this is ideal. And I must admit that it was quite nice not being concerned about being able to bring something home for dinner. However, the usual excitement of the hunt just wasn't there.

So in a quick recap, my walk with Christ had become stale and hunting wasn't very exciting either. This was true even though God was doing miraculous things in and through the ministry, and I had the privilege of hunting a prime piece of land.

Another book I was reading at that time was by Max Lucado and called *In the Grip of His Grace.* Basically Lucado said that when the mystery of something goes, so does the majesty. When we have the property and deer patterns figured out, the hunt is no longer a big deal. When we *think* we have God figured out, He's no big deal either. This is really a sad and lonely place to be.

If you combine my "rinse and repeat" weekly ministry activities with my lack of enthusiasm for hunting, I'm sure you sense just how dry my life was. My heart was in desperate need of change. I knew I was hungry, so like many good pastors, *eventually* I began to pray. As I've heard it put in the past, "I may not be fast, but at least I'm slow!" This good ol' boy finally got with the program.

That year a doe fell to my arrow early in the season. Then a 7-point whitetail. My heart was still numb, although I was praying for a revival in my soul. I bagged a 9-point during rifle season. Little did I know that this last buck would be a turning point in my life.

When I had completed field dressing the 9-pointer, I looked down at the gut pile and realized that much of what was lying on the ground was the same size as the organs in my body. This is when I sensed God putting His hand on my shoulder and speaking to my heart. As I continued to look down, He said that the difference between me and the deer was quite significant. "Even though things look the same, the deer has no place (organ) for My Holy Spirit to reside."

Immediately I felt set apart. The mystery and majesty of God returned to my life in a new and fresh way. Words and a concept so simple, yet they spoke directly to what I needed—a moment with the Master. Even now I can take you to the very spot of ground where this experience took place. My knee prints may still be there these 20 years or so later.

That was the first lesson I was aware of that God taught me while in the woods. And He has continued this method to this day. With pleasure I join Jay in sharing our trails with you. It is our prayer that this book will help you use your time in the woods to hunt *and* to experience special times with the Creator of the universe. He deeply wants a close relationship with you.

We encourage you to share the stories and experiences in this book with your family and friends as a wonderful way to grow in your faith together.

YOUR FIELD NOTES

Have you felt far from God? What was the circumstance?

How did you reconnect with the God who loves you?

When have you felt really close to the Lord? Where were you? What were you doing? Was anyone else around?

12

A Little About My Journey

Please allow me to confess something. One of the biggest issues I've had in my life is *not* viewing myself through God's eyes. Because of this, I never felt I was good enough for anyone or anything. I viewed myself as a failure. *I* didn't even want to be my friend, so why would God? And why would He want to answer any of my prayers?

This issue raised its head the first time when I was in the military. I was just starting out on the trail with Christ. I would read Mark 12:31—the "love your neighbor as yourself" verse—and then walk away thinking, "I need to love others more. I need to love others more. I need to work harder at this 'loving others' thing."

The churches I attended in the early days of my Christian life were great at communicating just how much of a depraved and selfish people we are. And if we're told something long enough, we begin to believe it…and act out what we believe, whether it's good or bad. Proverbs 23:7 tells us, "As he thinks in his heart, so is he" (NKJV). Ultimately, if we believe it, we will live it. This was my initiation into living a works-based Christian lifestyle.

To me, loving others more involved a couple of things. First, it meant never saying no to anyone who had any sort of need. I overextended myself in just about every area of my life as I helped people. I allowed my life to become so busy that I couldn't give any task enough time and energy to complete it to my satisfaction. Rushing from one place to another, I was also extremely critical of my performance. The poorly completed tasks further reinforced my sense of failure. "How could God love someone like me?" I thought. I felt like I couldn't even measure up to or please a *forgiving* God.

The other way I responded to others didn't have anything to do with them at all. If I couldn't love others more, I would compensate by loving myself less. Makes perfect sense, right? But this is a nasty road to go down. It's not hard to see where this line of thinking goes. It's also not hard to see that this type of mindset sets up footholds for the enemy to whisper lies into our hearts. "See how bad you are at the simple things? You can't do anything right. Certainly it's not good enough for God. After all, God is holy and perfect, right?" The lies became so deeply rooted in me that for many years I felt utterly unusable even by God. This line of thinking goes completely against Jesus' sacrifice on the cross and even His very nature. I know that now. However, when a heart is so deeply damaged and in need of repair, it's easy to embrace unbiblical theology. I knew enough not to apply this theology to others. I understood God loved everyone, so I figured I was squeaked in as part of the group.

After experiencing the pain of being overextended and feeling like such a failure, God took me back to the second foremost commandment as told by Jesus: "Love your neighbor as yourself" (Mark 12:31 NIV). I had neglected to include the last two words of the key portion of this passage: "as yourself." You mean it's all right to love me? *Yes, it is!*

As I travel around the country speaking at events these days, I'm no longer amazed to hear how many men feel the same way I did: unusable by God and not able to live approved by Him. The details may be different, but the end result is the same. Some people never feel good enough to be loved by God. They have bought a huge lie from the pit of hell.

Many thoughts, situations, and activities can lead us to not feeling good enough, but there is only one thing that can bring us out of it—God. "God demonstrates his own love for us in this: While we were *still* sinners, Christ died for us" (Romans 5:8 NIV). After my eyes were opened and my heart was healed, it was much easier to view myself from God's perspective. One by one He broke down the walls I'd erected with the devil's help. It was also much easier to hear His voice because I now understand He desires fellowship with me!

The bottom line is that my perspective of me doesn't matter. His perspective matters! His love is great enough that He died for me—whether I feel like I deserve it or not. "The LORD takes delight in his people" (Psalm 149:4 NIV).

YOUR FIELD NOTES

Have you been wounded enough that you feel God has to use you differently than He uses others? Explain.

How is God healing and restoring you?

13

Memories

My oldest son, Ken, and I were whitetail deer hunting on a piece of land we were very familiar with. I'd already taken two nice bucks out of this area, and hopefully it was Ken's turn. This would be his first deer.

We awoke early that frigid morning so we could be in place before the sun came up. Our routine was to leave early enough to stop for our traditional coffee and hot chocolate and make it to the woods in time for first light. This hunt was no different. After our coffee and hot chocolate and a short 20-minute drive, we arrived with 30 minutes to spare. We slipped into our ground blind and waited out the sunrise. We'd discovered this area was ripe for harvest when it came to does. We expected this hunt to be no different than the others—having a deer on the ground sometime before noon. But the day started out with no deer activity. We soon realized it was time to switch gears and try different tactics.

I wanted this hunt to be all about Ken getting his first deer, so now it was time to try pushing the deer out of their bedding areas. We made a plan. The wind was perfect for me to circle around the bedding area and push the deer his direction. All he had to do was let the deer pass him (to make sure I wasn't in his line of fire) and then take his shot. With that foolproof plan, I headed off to do my part.

Remember our traditional stop before our hunt? The one that included coffee and hot chocolate? Well, by this time of morning Ken's hot chocolate had run its course, and now he needed some relief. He tried to get my attention to stop me while he took care of business, but I had already disappeared into the trees. It was a pretty chilly morning and Ken was layered down with long-johns, sweat pants, and camo gear to stay warm. While I was beginning the slow trek through the trees, Ken was working to remove enough—well actually all—of his lower clothing.

Then he heard a noise. Being fully exposed, he wasn't prepared to take a shot. I'm sure you've seen comic portrayals of this type of situation at Bass Pro Shops or Cabela's. They can be found in the home decorating section of the store. You know the one I'm talking about— the painting of the hunter who got caught while trying to "take care of business" and is reaching for his rifle while a big buck prances by. If you've seen that picture, you've seen what happened to my son that day. Ken turned to see several does moving in his direction, and his gun was leaning against a tree.

So what did he do? He did what any respectable hunter would do. He picked up his gun and fired! I heard the shot but continued to push my way through the thicket just in case he'd missed. It was agonizing for me to continue my slow course. What if my son had taken his first deer? I wanted to be there for the excitement!

When I finally circled to where he was, I found him sitting on a log with a big grin on his face. "He knocked one down!" I thought. As I approached, a quick survey of the ground showed no deer down and no blood trail. I asked what had happened, and all he could do was laugh and say, "I had to shoot with my pants down!" Well, no deer that day for him, but we did get a great laugh out of the story. And, yes, I did buy him that painting from Bass Pro Shops the next time I went shopping for gear!

A number of years later, after we moved from Virginia to Colorado, Ken and I were on an archery elk hunt near Yampa, Colorado. We were in our camp trailer and listened to bull elk bugling all night long. Have you ever tried to get some sleep with that racket going on?

It was our second or third night of the hunt, and we were getting ready to shut things down for the evening. One last trip outside for a "bio break," and it was generator off and lights out. Ken went out one door, and I went out the other. We wanted to keep the heat in, so we quickly closed the trailer doors behind us. Ken finished first and headed back to the trailer. "Very funny," he called to me.

I had no idea what he was talking about. Ken can be a bit of a prankster, so when he said, "The door is locked!" I didn't think much of it. Besides, I knew I hadn't locked the door I'd gone out of. I thought, "Oh well, we have the other door. It's unlocked." Well, guess what? Both doors were locked! And the keys were on the counter inside. Here we were, both standing outside in our underwear at eleven o'clock at night in 20-degree weather. Ah, another fond hunting memory.

We sacrificed one of the slide-out windows on the trailer, and in I went to unlock one of the doors. This is a great time to mention that this is one reason why you should take a broadhead target when camping in a trailer. It happens to be just the right height to use to crawl through a window of an Outback trailer.

On another deer hunt with Ken, we used walkie-talkies to keep track of each other. He was in a treestand and I was on the ground on another ridge. We checked in every 30 minutes. During one of his check-ins he chattered like crazy. I asked him what all the talk was about and his response was "Bear!" Now it made sense. He was watching a bear, and it was getting a little too close for comfort. This was the first time he'd seen a bear in the wild, so it was understandable that he'd be nervous.

Why am I sharing all these stories? What are they about? Memories—memories that bring smiles to our faces and warmth to our hearts. For Ken and me, these stories are simple reminders that we've had fun times together. These father and son memories are sweet, and I wouldn't trade them for anything in the world. They bring pure joy to my heart. Our God loves us so much that He makes it possible for us to enjoy life!

Ken and I have these and many other memories for our enjoyment. What does God have? "Our Lord and God, You are worthy to receive glory and honor and power, because You have created all things, and because of Your will they exist and were created" (Revelation 4:11). He has you and me. I know that for some it's very hard to believe God delights in them, but He does! "The LORD your God is among you, a warrior who saves. He will rejoice over you with gladness. He will bring you quietness with His love. He will delight in you with shouts of joy" (Zephaniah 3:17).

YOUR FIELD NOTES

Take time to reflect on some of the great times you've had with friends and family. Share one or two of those stories. Include where you were, who you were with, and what happened.

Now share a great time you've had with God. Share what the circumstance was and why it was so special.

The Moment of Truth

When you squeeze the trigger or release an arrow the moment of truth about your preparation is only seconds away. How much work you put into getting ready for the hunt will become known. Will you hit or miss the target?

This reality isn't limited to hunting. This type of shot is executed many times each day before we go to the woods, to the office, or even get out of our bedrooms at home. Are you prepared with wisdom and guidance for the things you might run across today? "If any of you lacks wisdom, you should ask God, who gives generously to all without finding fault, and it will be given to you" (James 1:5 NIV). The word translated "wisdom" doesn't only apply to spiritual matters. It includes wisdom for life-related questions, work, home, and everywhere else. Experience tells a good hunter what to do in a given situation. When two bucks approach each other with their ears laid back, experience tells us what is about to happen. Experience can also tell us what to avoid.

When it comes to preparations, we reap what we've sown. If we've practiced hitting the target, the chances are really good we'll down something to eat when hunting. If we practice following God's principles, we'll experience His peace and blessings. But if we don't practice or consistently follow God, we'll also suffer the consequences. "Don't be deceived: God is not mocked. For whatever a man sows he will also reap" (Galatians 6:7-8). The Good News Bible paraphrases this verse:

"Do not deceive yourselves; no one makes a fool of God. You will reap exactly what you plant."

In our moments of truth, we'll be successful and content if we believe and act on Psalm 119:73-81 (NIV):

> Your hands made me and formed me;
> give me understanding to learn your commands.

> May those who fear you rejoice when they see me,
> for I have put my hope in your word.

> I know, LORD, that your laws are righteous,
> and that in faithfulness you have afflicted me.

> May your unfailing love be my comfort,
> according to your promise to your servant.

> Let your compassion come to me that I may live,
> for your law is my delight.

> May the arrogant be put to shame for wronging me
>   without cause;
> but I will meditate on your precepts.

> May those who fear you turn to me,
> those who understand your statutes.

> May I wholeheartedly follow your decrees,
> that I may not be put to shame.

> My soul faints with longing for your salvation,
> but I have put my hope in your word.

═══ YOUR FIELD NOTES ═══

Have you planned your shot at this life with careful consideration?

Have you accepted Jesus Christ as your Lord and Savior? If so, where were you, what was happening, who was with you?

Have your children accepted Christ as their Lord and Savior? If yes, write down what you know of their experiences.

As an added bonus, why not have your children who have accepted Christ write down their experiences or tell you about it so you can write it down in their words? Keep this information someplace safe so you can pass their testimonies on to them when they are older.

15

Nose to Nose

It was opening day of whitetail archery season in Virginia. I was positioned with my back against a barbed wire fence at the northeast corner of a horse pasture. To the north and east were thick short pines. To the west and south were young oaks. In the center was a lush green pasture. As the sun rose, I kept a watchful eye but I saw and heard nothing. Out came my grunt call and antlers. I grunted and waited a few minutes. Then I gave a little rattle with the antlers. Still I saw and heard nothing. Thirty minutes went by and nothing changed. An hour and still nothing. When I was just about to move to another spot, I thought I heard a noise behind me…like *right* behind me.

━━━━━━━━━━━ **YOUR FIELD NOTES** ━━━━━━━━━━━

Have you been in this position? When you're so convinced you heard or saw something so you were ready to shoot…only to find out that it was a bird landing on a limb, or a leaf falling to the ground, or even a pesky squirrel? Describe the incident.

Well, since there hadn't been any activity for so long, I didn't expect anything at this moment either.

YOUR FIELD NOTES

I've experienced this when it comes to prayer too. Have you? You've asked God for something, but you don't really expect Him to answer? Describe one of those times and include what happened.

I slowly turned around. I moved so incrementally that it seemed like it took me forever just to look over my shoulder. I didn't expect to see anything, but if there was I sure didn't want to spook it!

I froze. There I was, nose to nose with a 6-point buck. He was so close I could feel his breath! Picture this. I was sitting on the ground, my back against a wire fence, my head turned as far to the side as it could go. The curious buck had his nose right up against the fence behind me. We were no more than 24 inches apart! What a sight! In a flash and at the same time, we both let out snorts that could be heard for miles! Well, okay, maybe not miles, but if you come nose to nose with a deer like that, just see what noises you make! I'm not sure who was shocked the most—the buck or me.

Isn't it interesting how we prepare for something, and then sometimes we freak out when it happens? I think we're like that with God at times. We position ourselves in a certain place. We prepare ourselves. We pray. And when He answers our prayers, we are shocked! We are so stunned by the fact that He answered that we're not ready to act.

YOUR FIELD NOTES

Can you think of a time when you prayed, He answered, and you were so surprised you weren't ready to respond to His blessing? Describe the time, the circumstance, and why you weren't prepared.

Do you believe God truly cares about you? Why or why not? How does that affect how you pray?

What have you learned from prayers that it seems like God hasn't answered?

Do you pray with an expectation based on His character, on who He is? If yes, what specifically do you base your expectation on? Are there certain words or phrases you use that reveal your expectation that He will answer?

16

Facing the Challenges

A dear friend of mine, Larry Money, is the executive director of a retreat center a few miles north of Woodland Park, Colorado. Larry and Melody, his wife, have well over 400 acres of retreat property surrounded by the Pike National Forest. Coyotes, mule deer, mountain lions, black bears, elk, and the occasional turkey hang out in the surrounding landscape. What an office setting to have!

For 10 years Larry was on the hunt for a bull elk to mount and hang over the fireplace in their cabin. He took several cows through the years, but a bull evaded his crosshairs. Until this past season. I was hoping to hear the details of his hunt, so I called Larry. Melody answered the phone. As she gave me her side of the story, it was quite obvious that she was very proud of her husband.

Melody explained how it was one of those perfect situations—the wind was in their faces and the herd was at ease and felt unpressured. Melody explained, "Larry made a perfect shot. He put the crosshairs on the bull's vitals, controlled his breathing, and squeezed off the shot." She went on to say that afterward Larry said he was shaking in his boots. But one part of Melody's story struck me right between the eyes. As she explained how nervous Larry said he was, she described how rock steady he appeared to be. What really got me was what she said next: "I was right behind him praying." That Melody was praying wasn't surprising because that's her nature. She was right there with Larry.

We all need to be in close relationships with others who are committed to our success. We need family and close friends who will stand with us when things get tough, and even when it may hurt. When it comes to close friends, Bill Sanborn, Jay Houston, and my oldest son, Ken, are men I depend on when it comes to succeeding. By success I'm not referring to the entrepreneurial, go make lots of money type. What I'm talking about is success against the adversary who wants to keep us from succeeding in accomplishing what God has set before us. Success in areas that include parenting, being an effective employer or employee, teaching Sunday school, being a thoughtful spouse. And this is only a short list of targets in our lives the enemy—the devil—loves to focus on.

In regard to knowing God's will, one thing I've learned is to change my view of what it means when I ask God to open doors where He wants me to go and close those that lead to where He doesn't want me to go. The problem with this approach is that it implies that following God's calling will be easy...an easy trail because of the opened and closed doors. But this is not always true.

We don't have to travel very far into the Old Testament to see that challenges and following God often go hand in hand. Joshua experienced this at the battle of Jericho. "Now Jericho was strongly fortified because of the Israelites—no one leaving or entering. The Lord said to Joshua, 'Look, I have handed Jericho, its king, and its fighting men over to you'" (Joshua 6:1-2). When we read, "I have handed Jericho...over," it's easy to jump to the conclusion that it was going to be a "walk in and take over" assignment that wouldn't require much effort on Joshua's part.

God directed Joshua to have his men circle the city for six days: "March around the city with all the men of war, circling the city one time. Do this for six days" (6:3). Keep in mind that Jericho was a fortified city. I wonder what was going through the minds of the men? I'm sure they felt completely exposed as they marched around the city.

There are plenty of other examples where God's calling required something more painful or stressful than the obedience at the battle of Jericho. Consider Jesus in the garden of Gethsemane. His sweating drops of blood equals high stress! Jesus understood the need to have people close to Him to hold Him up when follow through on His calling was going to be difficult. This is why He was so grieved when He found His disciples sleeping: "He came to the disciples and found them sleeping. He asked Peter, 'So, couldn't you stay awake with Me one hour? Stay awake and pray, so that you won't enter into temptation. The spirit is willing, but the flesh is weak'" (Matthew 26:40-41).

Paul wrote that "our battle is not against flesh and blood, but against the rulers, against the authorities, against the world powers of this darkness, against the spiritual forces of evil in the heavens" (Ephesians 6:12). We have an adversary who is very interested in keeping us from accomplishing the tasks God sets before us. Where would we be if Jesus had said, "This is just too hard. If the Father was in this, it wouldn't be so difficult," and so He walked away?

YOUR FIELD NOTES

What has God called you to that is difficult? Explain the task and what makes it hard.

Who are the people who are praying for you and encouraging you?

Who are you praying for and encouraging?

What battles have you taken on or waged on behalf of your spouse or children or friends? Explain one of the situations and how you took action.

17

Bless What I Do?

One of the wonderful things about elk hunting with a bow in Colorado is that the season is approximately one month long and usually stretches from pre-rut to full-blown rut. The weather tends to be a little more comfortable for the archers than for "the rifle guys." The temperatures tend to range from the 20s to the 60s. This particular season was no different than any other (except this was the time Ken and I got locked out of the trailer).

Ken and I were hunting a piece of public land in the northwest corner of Colorado. It was full of great water sources and north-facing slopes where elk love to bed during the day. The excitement of listening to bulls bugling all night long, having a few close encounters, and our hunting days this season running out were hitting me in different ways.

We were down to our last few hours to hunt. It wouldn't be a stretch to say I was frustrated by time running short, elk close at hand, and not one beast had fallen to our arrows.

During this time I was in the process of writing a book about bowhunting in the backcountry, and I was hoping to get a good photo for the cover. This added pressure was really getting to me. It was sort of like the old saying "I want patience—and I want it now!" My prayers and thoughts were along the lines of "God, You know I need a book cover, so how 'bout it?" Isn't it funny how we pray more frequently and fervently when we want something specific?

My arrogant demands eventually softened and moved toward ones of dependence on God. "You know we don't have much time left in this season, Lord, and I certainly desire a nice bull for the book cover." This question may seem obvious to you, but it wasn't to me at the time: What if God doesn't want me to come up with a book cover photograph this year? No, I was all about furthering *my* agenda. Simply put, I had my plans and I wanted God to bless them.

As the final afternoon went on and the herds were beginning to make their way out of their bedding areas, I asked God for directions on where to go. Don't laugh! We've all been there—asking God for directions on which trees to place our treestands or where the best places are to set up blinds. In this case, I was looking at GPS coordinates, waiting for Him to tell me "down the hill" or "by the wallow you found yesterday." I was after specific directions to a specific location. What I got was silence. In trying to figure out God, I thought perhaps this was one of those times when "I've read the book so it's time to do what the book says."

At that moment God spoke. He challenged me in two areas. The first area concerned my prayer life. My passion to pray and seek Him more when it came to something I wanted was obvious. Was I praying about direction for daily life? I'd been doing things *for* Him, thinking that *He needed me* instead of asking Him about *what He wanted* to do in the world through me.

The second challenge came in the form of a question: "Do you want Me to bless what *you do* or do you want Me to *lead you* to the blessing?" At first glance this question looks pretty simple, but underneath the answer can be quite revealing. The first has to do with me simply wanting God to bless what I want, what my plans are. The second is all about me surrendering my will and goals to His agenda—His complete agenda. In my agenda I know what I want the outcome to be. With His I'm no longer in control.

We read that even Jesus never said anything on His own. He only spoke what the Father told Him: "I have not spoken on My own, but the Father Himself who sent Me has given Me a command as to what I should say and what I should speak" (John 12:49). If our desire is to model our lives after Jesus, this too should be the way we approach our lives. Now that we have the Holy Spirit—the Teacher—we have access to our heavenly Father's heart.

What other verses encourage us to live as Christ did? "Who among men knows the concerns of a man except the spirit of the man that is in him? In the same way, no one knows the concerns of God except the Spirit of God" (1 Corinthians 2:11). One of the roles of the Holy Spirit is to know the things that are on the Father's heart. Another role the Holy Spirit has is to teach us: "The Counselor, the Holy Spirit— the Father will send Him in My name—will teach you all things and remind you of everything I have told you" (John 14:26). "When the Spirit of truth comes, He will guide you into all the truth. For He will not speak on His own, but He will speak whatever He hears. He will also declare to you what is to come" (John 16:13). From these verses it's quite easy to see that the Holy Spirit puts on our heart what is on the Father's heart.

YOUR FIELD NOTES

What has the Holy Spirit placed on your heart?

When was the last time you asked Him to bless *your* plan? What was your plan, and what happened?

When was the last time you surrendered to Him, allowing Him to lead you to His blessing?

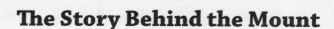

18

The Story Behind the Mount

Have you walked into a buddy's house and noticed one of his game mounts and thought, "Why in the world would he mount that? It's so small"? Or perhaps you thought, "Wow! Look at the size of that thing! It's huge!" Perhaps the small mount was his first deer or maybe it was his grandfather's. Maybe that particular animal was difficult to stalk or it was bagged the last day, the last hour of a long and hard season.

There is a story behind every mount. A tale that reminds the hunter of what took place in the process of getting that animal. The mount is a vivid reminder of the adventure of harvesting that critter. For the hunter, one look at the mount and the entire experience comes rushing back.

I've heard countless stories told and retold by hunters eager to share all the details of their hunts. As they tell the story, it's obvious they are reliving the event. Their ability to recall details can be amazing. The weather, the blisters, how far the shot was, who was with them, where they were—all details that make the story so interesting.

Interestingly, God instructed the Israelites to tell and retell their experiences the same way hunters do. To pass on to their descendants what they went through. And He had them leave physical reminders too. For instance, when the Israelites were piled up on the east side of the Jordan River and waiting to enter into the Promised Land, what did they do? God's instructions to Joshua were to have the people cross, and then have one member from each of the tribes of Israel take a stone from the middle of the Jordan River and place it where the Israelites were going to spend the first night. Notice when and where the stones were to be laid—*after* the crossing and *where others could see them.* This collection of stones would stand as a reminder to the current and future generations of what the Lord did: "This will be a sign among you. In the future, when your children ask you, 'What do these stones mean to you?' you should tell them, 'The waters of the Jordan were cut off in front of the ark of the LORD's covenant. When it crossed the Jordan, the Jordan's waters were cut off.' Therefore these stones will always be a memorial for the Israelites" (Joshua 4:6-7).

YOUR FIELD NOTES

The power of the story or testimony behind an event can be a powerful reminder of what was accomplished. What are some of the things you've seen God do in your life or the lives of others?

What items do you have that remind you of someone special or a special time or event? Give a brief description of the objects and share the story related to each one.

Describe each of these objects you've owned and give a brief story of an experience you've had involving them:

—a pocket knife:

—a shotgun:

—a picture:

19

Passing Wisdom On

A quick internet search shows that the wisdom behind the old saying of "values are caught not taught" can be applied to many aspects of life. Along with values, we can substitute in manners, truth, faith, and so on. I've been fortunate enough to do well in the archery world, but it didn't come easy. I've spent countless hours in the garage and at the archery range "paper tuning," working on my shooting form, and figuring out how to improve my scores and make the most of every shot opportunity. Because I've struggled but persevered, I've been blessed with fruit. I understand the value of passing on what I've discovered, and that adds even more enjoyment to the learning process.

During life we pass on all kinds of information, even when we're not doing it specifically. Our family members, friends, and those we encounter every day are "catching" things from us (hopefully not the flu!). We can also be deliberate and focused about what we pass on. Life is simply too precious to let the loved ones around us figure out all of life's aspects on their own. Our love for them drives us to intentionally pass on what we've discovered so they can avoid some of the pitfalls we've experienced and make it a point to experience the pluses we've found.

The apostle Paul was interested in passing along blessings: "I want very much to see you, that I may impart to you some spiritual gift to strengthen you" (Romans 1:11).

=========== **YOUR FIELD NOTES** ===========

Who has invested in you in a significant way? How did that person do it? How did you grow from that relationship?

Who would you like to spend more time with to benefit from his experience?

In what ways are you encouraging others?

Are your children growing strong because of your passion to pass on blessings that come from fathers?

Who would you like to spend more time with so you can teach or mentor him or her?

20

First Elk Hunt

Some of you may have read Jay Houston's *Elk Hunting 101, 201,* and *301* books. If you haven't, I highly recommend them. Jay has done a wonderful job of explaining basic to advanced elk hunting. I was fortunate enough to have been invited to contribute a chapter on back-country hunting in his *Elk Hunting 201* book. In that chapter I tell the story of the weekend my wife and I were scouting just prior to my first elk hunt during rifle season. During the first night of camping, we heard bull elk bugling up and down the narrow valley. We even had a small herd walk past our tent. Well, to be more accurate, I should say "around" our tent! We were surrounded by elk. Talk about exciting! Hearing their hooves crunch through the brittle ice and snow right outside our tent was exhilarating. After finding such a promising location, I planned to return the next weekend. My dreams of a successful first elk hunt soared.

Fast-forward four days. I headed back to the same campsite, except this time I was alone. It was shortly before sunset. I was setting up my tent when I noticed movement across the valley, about 150 yards to the west. I realized it was a cow moose with her calf coming to feed and water. Seeing this kind of activity was a good sign, but my adrenaline made sleeping that night a little difficult.

The next morning I headed to a spot I'd picked out and waited for my trophy elk to stroll by. A cute little mule deer doe meandered past at 20 yards, but that was it. Apparently the elk never got the invitation to the party. I stayed until I thought the elk were bedded down for the day, and then I headed out in search of tracks. It didn't take long to realize they'd circled around me by moving higher on the mountain. Not wanting to push them out of their beds and being a little worn out, I decided to retreat to my tent and make up for the short sleep time I'd had the night before.

A couple of hours of shut-eye and I was refreshed, so I headed back to my ambush point. What happened next sure hit me by surprise. After sitting for about 30 minutes, I became restless. Here I was deep in prime elk country on my first hunt, and my heart had become restless. A flood of emotion washed over me. Where had this come from? The beauty of the Gunnison Basin in central Colorado faded because all I could think about was "What's going on with me?" I couldn't sit still. On the edge of blubbering like a baby, I headed back to camp while asking the Lord about what I was experiencing.

What He revealed to me was interesting. For the past six years I hadn't been on a hunt without my oldest son, Ken. We were hunting partners, a father and son pair, great friends. I knew his thoughts without asking, and he knew mine. We could put a stalk on an animal with little communication. This time was different. Ken had moved to Wisconsin, so I was in a new chapter of hunting. I realized the emotion that had hit me so hard was that I was alone. I missed my huntin' buddy.

Ken has since moved back to Colorado, and we've picked up right where we left off. We've had encounters with badgers, elk, bear, squirrel, and mule deer. We've tried to have encounters with a host of other game as well. What we do have for all our adventures are great memories. Looking back, I understand my heart was grieving the temporary loss of the ability to create memories with someone else—especially my eldest son. We were made for relationships. We long for relationships with our Creator, the people we love, and with friends and acquaintances. Can you relate?

━━━━━ **YOUR FIELD NOTES** ━━━━━

Who do you have great memories of spending time with? What were you doing together?

How did that time together impact your life?

Whom has God put in your life to create memories with now? What is one of your most valued memories with that person?

21

Herd or Satellite Bull?

If you're after a bull elk, one choice you must make is whether to go after a herd bull or one of a herd's "satellite" bulls. If it's the herd bull you're after, usually the largest bull in the herd, there are hunting methods that will often yield an encounter with that bull. However, the tactics can come at a price. One choice is how a hunter goes about using an elk call.

Very aggressive "I want your cows" calling inside a bull's "trouble bubble" can produce a face-to-face confrontation with him. On the flipside, this tactic may shut down the bulls in surrounding herds, perhaps for days. Not wanting to risk the loss of their cows, the herd bulls may hear the aggressive sound of a new challenger and choose to go silent.

Although the aggressive calling may produce fewer encounters, they may generate encounters with bigger animals. For many, this risky approach has proven very effective. In 2009, it produced a 320-inch bull at 59 yards—pretty good by Colorado standards! I had to fully commit to luring him in.

This reminds me of when the Israelites headed out of Egypt. The priests carrying the ark of the covenant faced a similar situation—the need to commit—when crossing the Jordan River. Do you remember the story? Moses died so Joshua took command of the Israelites. It's time to enter the Promised Land (Joshua 3:1–4:24). One thing separates the Israelites from their destination: the Jordan River. And it was at flood stage (3:15).

The first to cross the river were the priests carrying the ark of the covenant (3:8). Ordinarily, crossing this river at flood stage was risky business. The river banks were steep and slippery. With the river in this condition, a full commitment to enter the water was required from each of the priests. They would have had to jump in! Joshua announced, "When the feet of the priests who carry the ark of the LORD, the Lord of all the earth, come to rest in the Jordan's waters, its waters will be cut off. The water flowing downstream will stand up in a mass" (3:13). There was no opportunity to test God a little at a time to see if He would truly stop the water. They had to boldly act, believing God would do His work.

Today we too often face times when God wants us to fully commit to Him. The times of testing the water are over, and we're to step out and trust Him fully.

YOUR FIELD NOTES

Where has the Holy Spirit been prodding you to fully commit? Has it been with trusting Him for employment? Perhaps with your speech or thoughts? Spending more time praying and getting to know Him? Spending more quality time with your family? Be specific. Include what you will do this week to commit more fully to what the Holy Spirit is calling you to do.

22

The First Time

I had the wonderful fortune of having a father and brother who owned airplanes, so I was exposed to aviation at a very young age. By high school graduation, I was blessed to have earned a commercial pilot license. As I neared graduation, my father had conversations with me (sometimes it felt like they were "at" me) about teaching flying while I was in college. Teaching was something I just wasn't interested in. You see, I'd worked all my life and finally made it to the pilot's seat. I didn't want to give that up and move back to the right seat and let someone else do the flying. I wanted to be in control! But I did end up doing some teaching, and I found it quite rewarding after all.

A few years ago I took over as the director of High Country Ministries (HCM), an outdoor ministry Jay Houston had started a number of years earlier. My partner, Randy Matthews, and I spoke to a local outfitter who jumped at the idea of donating fully guided and outfitted hunts to HCM. These hunts would be for youth. During hunting time, we set up one-on-one time with the kids and their dads to generate discussions, and any topic is allowed. Perhaps a son or daughter is dealing with peer pressure and wants advice. Maybe a father needs to confess something and ask for forgiveness.

One of the requirements the outfitter placed on Randy and me is that we would be guides for some of the hunters. Is your first thought, "How cool is that"? In reality, it can be very hard. Why? The hunts are conducted on private ranchland in eastern Colorado—the heart of record-class mule deer and antelope country. In fact, the outfitter has a great picture hanging in his bunkhouse of a 220-inch mule deer taken with a bow on that property. This makes it difficult to *not* be the one taking the shot. My attitude changed, though, after serving as a guide for my first father/daughter pair. I've found that just like teaching flying, the blessings I receive from guiding a son or daughter on a first hunt far outweighs the thrill of being the one who gets to squeeze the trigger. It's all about the investment, about being there to share in the experience. It's an amazing time. And in all the hunts we've conducted so far, only two people haven't filled their tags.

In the evening after hunting, we sit and listen to the group share their stories of crawling through cactus needles to put the "Mohican sneak" on pronghorns, the fastest land animals in North America, who also have incredible eyesight is incredible, is exciting! Trust me—a stalk in open terrain on what I call a 4-legged turkey (because of that astounding eyesight) is a real challenge!

My wife and I guided and invested early in our twins, Jake and Kylie. They accepted Christ as their Savior at the age of five. We didn't pressure them into taking communion because we wanted them to wait until they understood what it represents, what it's all about. That time came a few weeks ago.

Fast-forward to this past Sunday. This was the second time Kylie was going to take communion. She was sitting on my daughter-in-law's lap the entire service because she wanted to get the elements with her. Kylie is our "wiggly" one, so I kept a good eye on her as she walked back to her seat with the juice that could stain every pretty dress between us and the communion table. I've taken communion countless times through the years, but watching my daughter, whom I call "Sweetie," was special. I sat down and watched as Kylie carefully made her way back to her seat, protecting the bread and juice. It was one of the most precious and exciting things I've ever seen! It was thrilling to watch her take communion. To see my daughter embrace her relationship with Christ captured my heart in that moment and nearly took me to my knees. Oh my...words can't express what it meant to see my child make a connection this huge. All the "guiding" her mother and I had done had taken root. The fruit was an eternal relationship with her Creator and Savior!

This "guiding" has probably changed me more than it's changed those I've guided. Moving to the right seat in the airplane and being the one behind the binoculars instead of a rifle in the field has blessed me more than I can relate.

YOUR FIELD NOTES

Do you have stories about how your guidance has blessed someone? Share an instance or two. Who were you with and what were you doing?

How are you guiding your children to prepare them for life?

Are you guiding or helping guide others? What are you doing, who are you helping, and why are you choosing to be involved?

How has guiding others blessed you?

23

A Little Fun

I can become very focused when it comes to filling my game tags. Maybe there is a specific animal I'm after to complete a grand slam. Perhaps I know my days in the woods will be limited because of family or work commitments—or even pending weather. The thing that really pushes me is the stress of the season coming to a close when I haven't gotten my animal. Oh the pressure! These things really crank up the heat and my drive.

Bearing this in mind, now add the element of a young hunter. Recently one of my young ones at home said, "I want to go hunting too!" Ordinarily I'd be delighted, but there was that pressure to get an animal on the ground…to bring home dinner. On this particular occasion it involved turkeys.

I'm not sure why I waited, but I didn't take up turkey hunting until I moved to Colorado. Just so you know, Colorado is *not* the best place to learn how to hunt turkeys. It's sort of like growing up in Africa, then moving to New York City, and only then deciding to hunt rhinos. Back in my days in the military I was in prime locations for turkey, but I didn't have the interest then. Go figure. So fast-forward to today. Now I've been bitten by the turkey bug, and the western birds are some of the most difficult to bag.

I was down to four days left in the spring season, but I only had two days available. I loaded up the truck Wednesday night, and Thursday morning I was on the road for a two-hour drive to a new hunting spot. As I got closer to my destination, the clouds got darker and lower. The temperature dropped. It was in the 50s when I'd left the house, but now it was in the upper 30s. It rained. Before I could get off the interstate, the temperature had dropped even more and the rain had turned to hail. Yep—hail, not snow. And I still had another hour to drive. What would any reasonable hunter do? Turn around and head home! Hail in Colorado is associated with one thing: thunderstorms. Thunderstorms in the high country are dangerous! But my sometimes fanatical drive to fill my tag kept me focused. I continued on.

When I arrived at the trailhead, it was snowing, hailing, and visibility was barely 50 yards. Thunder and lightning were booming and striking everywhere. Wisdom suddenly came, and I never even got out of my truck. I headed home, sad but comforted by the fact that I'd given it one last try.

At home later my wife mentioned that our daughter had a birthday party to go to this week, and our son wasn't invited. My brain quickly leaped into gear. Jake and I could spend time together while Kylie and my wife were at the party!

With an unfilled turkey tag and a six-year-old son who wanted to go hunting, I had a decision to make. Would the hunt focus on turkey (really me) or would I work at giving Jake a terrific Saturday in the mountains with his dad? I chose the latter. This was going to be a father/son day. If we saw a bird, fine, but it would not be the primary focus of our time together.

We arrived at the same location I'd been at two days earlier. We unloaded the ATV and down the trail we went. We'd stop occasionally to look for turkey tracks, do a little turkey calling, and just sit and chat. Jake was my focus, not bagging a turkey. We also found lots of elk tracks so we discussed the differences between bulls, cows, and calf tracks. We also found very fresh bear scat, which opened a new discussion.

We had a really enjoyable father/son time. I think the highlight of the trip was when Jake asked if he could shoot his Airsoft pistol he'd brought along. We were down by a stream, and he was firing rounds like it was the War of 1812! Little yellow pellets were splashing into the water like a World War II dogfight over the Pacific. Until Jake saw a beetle on a log. With great patience and accuracy, he aimed and squeezed the trigger. The beetle was history! He hit the little critter. The grin on his face was priceless! On the way home that night, we stopped for our usual post-hunt pizza.

"Dad, tell the waitress about my beetle!" Jake said. He was so proud! We even joked about having it mounted. That was one Saturday I wouldn't trade for any bearded tom!

YOUR FIELD NOTES

Have you experienced target fixation? Has your drive for harvesting an animal been so great you overlooked something important? If yes, explain.

Is there someone in your life who could use a beetle hunt? If not your own kids, how about the son or daughter of a single mom in your church? Or a grandchild? Jot down a name or two, write down a plan, and then make it happen.

24

Resolve and Character

I have a long list of hunters and sportsmen I respect and even envy because of their list of trophies taken, including Fred Bear, Bob Foulkrod, Danny Farris, Chuck Adams, and David Blanton. These men have taken countless numbers of animals throughout their careers. There is one thing all of these men have in common: resolve. And I have a dear friend I've added to this list, Marc Smith of Wild Country Outdoors. He's almost made me jealous some years. He brings home a big bull elk and large mule deer every year. Without fail, Marc bags great animals every time he heads to the mountains. Why have these men been so successful? Again, it's resolve.

Marc determines beforehand to do whatever it takes to legally get the animal he's after. A few years ago, Marc was after a particular muley. His hunt was originally scheduled for five days, but that was just not getting the job done. He extended his scheduled time on the mountain for an additional five days. For 10 days he chased this mule deer. Keep in mind that Marc had prepared for a *five-day hunt*. The cost of his resolve? A shortage of food. Why would he put himself in such a position? He'd found the buck he wanted, and it was taking him much longer to fill his tag.

In Colorado, once you find the particular animal you're after in the high country, it's wise to stay on that animal until you've put it on the ground. Marc knows this, and coming off the mountain to replenish his supplies was too time-consuming. There are plenty of small game animals in season during the archery deer season, and it's quite common for bowhunters to also purchase a small game license just in case an opportunity presents itself to take a grouse for food. That is exactly what Marc did. While he ate his share of grouse and grubs that fall, he also brought home one of his biggest mule deer ever.

When it comes to hunters, I respect Marc. When it comes to men of faith, I have a long list of men I deeply respect as well, including Billy Graham, James Dobson, Chuck Swindoll, and Henry Blackaby. These men have resolved to protect their character at all cost. They understand that character matters. They also know that character comes before the calling, and they have put measures in place to ensure they remain clean. They have resolved to stay the course God has placed in front of them.

Often in our walk with Christ, we are tempted to "come off the mountain" when the going gets tough. Can you relate?

YOUR FIELD NOTES

When have you been tempted to "come off the mountain" early yet chose to remain? What were the circumstances? What made you stay the course? Was the outcome what you hoped?

25

The Simple Joys

Occasionally I find myself researching a new gadget that promises to take my hunting to the next level or add a new dimension. Sometimes I find myself thinking of the early days when the American settlers couldn't go down to Cabela's to get the latest waterproof clothing. They didn't have access to chemicals that would keep their human scent under control. Yet they didn't starve. They did just fine with weapons that were much more primitive than today's gear. Maybe going back to the basics wouldn't be so bad. After all, when we have less to rely on we become better hunters.

Although it may be more difficult to hunt with older, less sophisticated equipment, the challenge can yield much more satisfaction when the hunt is over. In the same way, life is much more satisfying when we yield to the Maker of the universe. We need to allow Him to equip us as He sees fit.

I shot competitive archery for several years and greatly enjoyed it. Perhaps the part that I enjoyed most was the required precision. In the class I shot in, "unlimited," to be competitive the archer needs to be able to consistently group his arrows within a one-inch circle. This demanded constant focus and attention to the details of my equipment. Every step in my 16-step shot process had to have a purpose and be followed carefully.

Through the years I slowly realized that, while competitive archery was still enjoyable, it wasn't always very much fun. The seriousness of competition had taken its toll. Archery became fun again when I picked up a longbow. For those who don't know, a longbow basically is a straight stick and a string. No fancy cams and high-tech risers. Just a wooden stick and a string.

When I practiced at the archery range with my target compound bow, I was disappointed if my arrow hit outside a one-inch group. When shooting a longbow, I was thrilled to hit the target!

YOUR FIELD NOTES

What in your life has required so much attention that it's taken away some of the simple joy in life? How does it manifest?

What can you do to experience again the simple joys of life?

When was the last time you spent quality time with friends who matter most to you? What did you do?

Describe the last time you spent quality time with your wife, son, or daughter. What made the time special?

26

Dwell

I know several hunters who are very quick to study the terrain and get their treestand hung in a prime location prior to deer season. I know others who are in the woods building an elaborate ground blind so they can be in a perfect spot on opening day. They want to get their stand or blind established before others stake a claim to their spots. They want to be assured of a good place to "dwell" during the season. They've taken valuable time to enter the next season prepared. When the time for hunting begins, they arrive at their stands long before daylight. Because they've studied the area, they know what to expect when daylight arrives.

Colossians 3:16 says, "Let the message about the Messiah dwell richly among you, teaching and admonishing one another in all wisdom, and singing psalms, hymns, and spiritual songs, with gratitude in your hearts to God" (Colossians 3:16). The word "dwell" means to inhabit a fixed position. The Message Bible paraphrases it this way: "Let the Word of Christ—the Message—have the run of the house." Making an effort is required to establish a good place to dwell during hunting season, and the same is true with making sure God's Word dwells in our hearts.

I'm sure you've seen people who head out to hunt with little or no preparation. Typically they don't bring much home. So it is with God's Word. I've been quick to dive right in, read a few verses, and then be on my way…not stopping to ponder what I just read. Not giving the Holy Spirit time to penetrate my heart with His wisdom. Psalm 46:10

puts it in this convicting way, "Stop your fighting—and know that I am God, exalted among the nations, exalted on the earth." Stop fighting whom? God! Spend time with Him in His Word. If you don't, your spiritual time will yield the same results as going into the woods without preparation.

=== **YOUR FIELD NOTES** ===

Are you prepared for "daylight"? What more can you do to be ready?

Take time right now to ask God to guide you through the thorns and thickets of life. Why not write out your prayer?

Who are you hunting with—in the field and in your spiritual life? How do you encourage each other?

27

Finding the Treasure

New hunting products come out every year. If you're like me, when in the woods you discover a shortfall in your equipment and think, "It sure would be nice if I had a piece of equipment that would...." For example, the temperature changes experienced while hunting in the high country of the West can be astounding. I've been through nights where temperatures dipped into the teens and the high for the day soars into the 70s. Hunters start with long-johns and then wish they had cut-offs on by noon. I think, "Wouldn't it be nice to have a comfortable pack that doesn't make my back sweat?" Or when I'm in my treestand I think, "Wouldn't it be nice to have equipment that doesn't creak?" Has the wool from your mitten gotten caught on the thumb safety of your rifle while the deer you wanted to shoot watched? Has your arrow fallen off the rest just as you were halfway to full draw on a royal bull elk? Yep, we start making mental lists of the things that will make our hunt next week or next year more successful and comfortable.

Then *it* happens. Catalogs start coming in the summer. Isn't it fun to look through all those advertisements that come in the mail prior to hunting season? We dream, plan, search for new pieces of equipment that have been developed since the last hunting season. We spend hours reading reviews and asking others about this or that item. Then we find it! You know, that new product that hits your heart and promises to make next season a success. You dwell on it, thinking about how you could have used it last year and what a difference it will make this year.

Would you like to ask God a question that will grab His heart every time? A question that He longs to hear? A question that will bring His heart closer to yours? Ask Him, "What can I use today that will help my life more significantly further the gospel of Christ?" Browsing through magazines and catalogs has its place, but it should never take precedence over drawing closer to Christ and fulfilling His call on your life. Matthew 6:21 says, "Where your treasure is, there your heart will be also." Just maybe it's time to put down the magazines and catalogs and see what wisdom God would like to give you through His Word.

YOUR FIELD NOTES

What plan can you implement to help you spend more consistent, quality time with God?

What is your plan to ensure that your family is doing the same?

How have you been encouraged by God as you've spent time alone with Him?

28

The Right Perspective

I've known many hunters who don't know how to read a map or use a compass. I've discovered this many times over and even had it confirmed during conversations with hunters. It's easy to fall into a sense of complacency because we stay close and usually know the land. Is this okay? After all, we can get turned around so easily, accidents happen, and hunts don't always go as planned. A coworker used to go with his buddies to Colorado every year to hunt elk. One particular year he got lost, and he wasn't prepared to spend the night away from camp. He was cold and wet—two potentially dangerous states. The next morning, thankfully, he found his way back to camp. That overnight hike taught him a few good lessons. Don't let your socks get too close to the fire (his were torched while trying to dry them out). Know basic survival skills. Know where you are at all times. As it turned out, he was only 1.5 miles from his campsite and fellow hunters.

A close friend, Craig Glass, conducts men's retreats around the country for Peregrine Ministries. Many of these are father/son retreats that focus on the fathers passing their wisdom and blessing on to their sons. There is one illustration that Craig uses that is very powerful. He has all of the sons remain in their cabins while the fathers place obstacles on a narrow bridge over a creek. Each obstacle represents a challenge the father has experienced in his life—things the father has tripped over relationally, morally, and spiritually. Each son is then blindfolded, and his father leads him across the bridge. The blindfold requires the son to place his trust in his father's hands. As they come to each obstacle the father explains or confesses what it represents and what he is doing now to avoid each of the obstacles. How the father navigates each obstacle may include mentioning who is helping him as well.

YOUR FIELD NOTES

How are you preparing for your next hunt?

How are you passing your life lessons on to others?

Who are you helping navigate life?

How are you guiding those around you so they don't fall to the temptations you succumbed to?

A Strong Heart

Wouldn't it be nice to climb into your treestand only minutes before a trophy buck comes walking out of a thicket at a distance of 20 yards? And be broadside too? Treestand hunting is certainly a waiting game much of the time. Perhaps "endurance" is another word that accurately describes this type of hunting. Sometimes another word that goes with hunting is "discouragement." Hours pass with little or no excitement or encouragement.

Seasons of life can be like hunting too. There are times that seem like "waiting" is the only goal, and there's no hope of encouragement. However, God's Word has a few things to say about this:

> Wait for the LORD; be courageous and let your heart be strong. Wait for the LORD (Psalm 27:14).

> I wait for the LORD; I wait, and put my hope in His word (Psalm 130:5).

> Be strong and courageous, for you will distribute the land I swore to their fathers to give them as an inheritance (Joshua 1:6).

> So we must not get tired of doing good, for we will reap at the proper time if we don't give up (Galatians 6:9).

Seasons of life that seem to bring lessons of waiting for Him can be a little discouraging at times. These times can feel like they're sucking the energy and hope out of us. I've even wondered if God remembered I was still around. He always does though. "Brothers, do not grow weary in doing good" (2 Thessalonians 3:13). For the word translated "weary," Paul used the Greek word *ekkakeo*, which describes being utterly spiritless. And that's a good description of how I've felt at times.

So where can we find help in getting out of a funk? There are a couple of verses that speak to this. Let's go back to Galatians 6:9: "So we must not get tired of doing good, for we will reap at the proper time if we don't give up." "Proper time" indicates a time that is decisive and unique. In other words, it's specific to us right now. Paul also wrote, "Keeping our eyes on Jesus, the source and perfecter of our faith, who for the joy that lay before Him endured a cross and despised the shame, and has sat down at the right hand of God's throne" (Hebrews 12:2). If we combine these two verses, we see that Jesus is "authoring" what we believe. He is using life experiences to craft what we believe, what our convictions are. "Let us run with endurance the race that is set before us, fixing our eyes on Jesus, *the author and perfecter of faith*" (Hebrews 12:1 NASB).

YOUR FIELD NOTES

Waiting to receive encouragement can be very lonely. Who are you encouraging right now, reminding him that Jesus is always present and His timing is perfect?

Who has been an encouragement to you in this way? What was the situation, and how did this person help you?

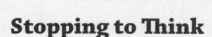

30

Stopping to Think

One of the biggest challenges with elk or mule deer hunting is the animals aren't as predictable as whitetails. One factor for unpredictability is the weather. A drought can dramatically change where the animals can be found. Many western hunters know that scouting is incredibly important, and where a hunter scouts should be driven by the summer and fall moisture patterns. However, I know hunters who don't stop to think about how the summer rain may have affected where the animals are located. They know the animals were in a particular location three years ago, so they assume they'll be there every year. This can be a big waste of time!

Not stopping to think through things in life can be even more detrimental. There was a time in my life when I tended to act impulsively. I didn't stop to consider the possible consequences of my actions. This can be dangerous in relationships, the work environment, and other aspects of life. Where did this tendency come from? When I was growing up (and after I'd reached the age where spankings no longer were effective) and got into trouble, I'd be disciplined by being sent to my room with the admonition: "Think about what you've done, and when you're finished you can come out of your room." After I'd thought about it a while, I could come out and life was back to normal. The problem was that I was still pretty young and didn't have the understanding to wisely think through the issues. In the long run, this taught me that thinking through anything equated to being punished, so I refused to think things through. Many of my actions were impulsive, and I often paid the price for them.

YOUR FIELD NOTES

When it comes to raising children, do you think through your actions with and around them? How are you impulsive and how are you deliberate during the times you spend with them?

Are you choosing (or helping them choose) the movies they watch, the games they play, and the outside influences they have? What standards do you use?

What are some steps you can take to ensure that you and your children are thinking through each decision?

And what do you do about situations when you need to make a decision and you don't have much knowledge about the subject matter?

James 1:5 offers us great advice:

> Now if any of you lacks wisdom, he should ask God, who gives to all generously and without criticizing, and it will be given to him. But let him ask in faith without doubting. For the doubter is like the surging sea, driven and tossed by the wind. That person should not expect to receive anything from the Lord. An indecisive man is unstable in all his ways.

The word translated "wisdom" in this verse is the Greek word *sophia*. *Strong's Exhaustive Concordance* provides this definition: "wisdom, broad and full intelligence; used of the knowledge of diverse matters." In other words, it applies to any kind of wisdom.

31

Danger, Risk, Faith

Stories we hear and television shows we watch that show successful hunts done deep in dangerous territory excite our senses and really get our blood pumping. If the hunt takes place in grizzly bear country, there is an added element of danger that keeps us on the edge of our seats. What must it be like being there? Our level of adrenaline flow rests on the perceived amount of risk, especially when we're unsure of the outcome. The *Merriam-Webster* definition of "risk" is: "someone or something that creates or suggests a hazard." I don't know about you, but I sure think a grizzly nearby "suggests a hazard"!

While this seems to hold true for stories of adventure, what about situations involving God where we're unsure of the outcome? What if God called you to something out of the ordinary, something out of your comfort zone? Would you shrug it off, thinking it couldn't be from God? After all, you're not qualified for the task since you don't have experience. Perhaps He's calling you to go into vocational ministry. Maybe He is leading you to take a lower-paying job or even to go on a mission trip.

One thing I know is that we human beings like certainty. We want to know the outcome *before* we'll commit. Imagine considering hiring an outfitter to take you on an Alaskan moose hunt. Before spending $10,000, you'd like to know if it's a guaranteed hunt, right? This approach to life can present some challenges when it comes to a faith-based relationship with God.

Let's dissect Hebrews 11:6 a little bit: "Now without *faith* it is impossible to please God, for the one who draws near to Him must believe that He exists and rewards those who seek Him." There are many aspects of this verse we could unpack, such as pleasing God. However, for now, let's focus on one thing: faith. The word translated "faith" comes from the Greek word *peitho,* a verb that means "to trust, have confidence, to obey." In other words, *faith requires action based on trust.* The outcome is God's responsibility. Our responsibility is simply to obey Him.

Imagine how Abraham must have felt when God instructed him to take his beloved son Isaac to Mt. Moriah to present him as a burnt offering (Genesis 22:2). Or what do you think Gideon thought about the size of his army when God got through? Gideon's army was facing the Midianite army, believed to number nearly 135,000 men (Judges 8:10). Gideon started with 32,000 men (Judges 7:2-3). After God whittled them down, Gideon only had 300 warriors left (Judges 7:6). Military strategists would think this decrease in numbers crazy and suicidal. Why would God do something so unreasonable? So only He would receive the glory! It may be a stretch that 32,000 men could defeat 135,000. However, 300 against 135,000? Only God could do something like that! Many of the assignments God gives us are God-sized, meaning tasks that only He can accomplish. Assignments that leave room for only God to receive the glory.

Trusting God for your next assignment should be more thrilling than an Alaskan moose hunt! Faith means you don't control the outcome—God does. What He says He'll do is guaranteed to be completed:

> So the LORD gave Israel all the land He had sworn to give their fathers, and they took possession of it and settled there. The LORD gave them rest on every side according to all He had sworn to their fathers. None of their enemies were able to stand against them, for the LORD handed over all their enemies to them. None of the good promises the LORD had made to the house of Israel failed. Everything was fulfilled (Joshua 21:43-45).

YOUR FIELD NOTES

What God-sized assignment are you being called to?

How do you see God leading you?

What are your fears about the assignment?

How are you going to proceed?

32

Lesson or Frustration?

The 2010 Colorado archery elk season was a complete bust for many hunters. The season started out in early September, as usual, with bull elk bugling and fighting to establish dominance in their territories. The bulls were right on schedule; the cows were not. The cows usually come into heat near the middle of September, with the male rut in full swing by late September.

What was so different about 2010? In short, the weather. Most believe that the dynamics of a drastic drop in temperature or foul weather moving in kick the animals into gear and get the hormones moving. However, this isn't so. What starts the estrus cycle for the cows is the amount of sunlight, which is registered through the cows' eyes. This is the same thing that causes bucks and bulls to lose their antlers in the spring, that starts antler regrowth, and that ends antler growth. This is also what causes the bulls to fight for dominance when they do.

Colorado weather patterns from spring to late summer were the usual. The bulls established their dominance as normal. However, when mid-September arrived, Colorado didn't experience the usual weather pattern changes. The overcast, rainy days in the high county, which effectively shorten the amount of daylight (read sunlight) never happened. Beautiful, clear, blue sky days occurred during late September. With the lack of reduced sunlight, the cows' bodies weren't kicking into estrus. And it's when the cows are in heat that hunters can take advantage of the breeding instincts of bulls. Since the cows weren't ready for breeding, the bulls weren't excited. Instead of bugling, they were silent.

This made finding elk by sound extremely difficult. With the much higher than normal temperatures—93 degrees at 13,000 feet—the elk stayed bedded down during the daylight hours. Only after sunset, well after shooting light was gone, did the elk move out to feed.

As this scenario unfolded, I had a choice to make from two options. I could get frustrated, upset, and disappointed. Or I could be grateful for the opportunity to learn something new. I chose the second one. What I learned in 2010 already has me wondering about the 2011 season. So far Colorado experienced an unusually sunny spring, and the mule deer have already begun to grow their antlers (two to three months early). I normally plan to hunt the rut in late September, but this year I may want to hunt earlier, when the bulls are establishing dominance.

YOUR FIELD NOTES

Describe a time when you had the opportunity to grow from a hunting situation. What are the details?

How can you help others grow in their hunting and spiritual endeavors?

33

Making Memories

A dear friend of ours, Andy Andrews, asked if my eldest son, Ken, and I wanted to go squirrel hunting. It took no time to answer with an excited "Yes!" Ken and I talked and made plans for the weekend hunt a few days away. The plan was to drive to western Virginia Friday night, set up camp, and be ready to go Saturday morning.

The week couldn't go fast enough. That is, until it was time to leave Friday night. The weather was nasty, to say the least, with high winds and heavy rain. But those weren't the bad parts. It was the flooding and lightning that really dampened my desire to go after those furry little things. But Andy is one of those guys who have a fun time no matter what the weather is. I wanted to wait out the storm, but he convinced us to go anyway.

Two hours later we arrived at the campsite. Fortunately, we were on high enough ground that flooding wasn't a threat. However, lightning was still flashing all around us. I was acting like a Grumpy Gus when Andy looked at me and said, "Makin' memories!" and laughed. *Bah humbug,* I thought. I went through my mental list of reasons I didn't want to get my down sleeping bag wet, how uncomfortable we'd all be soaking wet in 40-degree weather, and that we would have nothing dry enough to start a fire. I was even convinced the tent would leak.

We got the tent pitched, all of our gear inside, and were fast asleep in no time. I awoke the next morning expecting to be soaked to the bone and cold. However, I was neither. In fact, I was dry, warm, and rested. We all were. Now "makin' memories" is a phrase I use to get myself perked up.

That morning we hunted our hearts out and never got a single squirrel. But we did come home with memories!

═══════════ **YOUR FIELD NOTES** ═══════════

When was the last time you wanted to stay in a "stick in the mud" way, but you ended up enjoying yourself? What were you doing, and who was with you?

How did that change how you respond to situations now?

34

Where To?

One of the most frequent questions I get when doing seminars is, "How can I know where all the animals are?" When hunting, we're all interested in knowing this! It sure would make life easier if we knew exactly where to go each time we hit the woods or fields. I admit that I've even asked God for guidance on where to find animals. And I'm sure I'm not the first to ask Him this! You know, "God, GPS coordinates would be nice…"

The most unproductive and inefficient way to find animals is to wander around in the woods. If you stumble across your quarry, you never know if it was your skill or happenstance. Plus roaming around is a great way to push animals out of the area.

The men I speak to in churches want to know something equally important: how to know what God is calling them to. Knowing where to go in life is one of the biggest questions our hearts yearn to have answered. We want to know we were made for a purpose, that our births weren't mistakes, that we really do matter. When I give advice at a hunting seminar, I'm providing what I *believe* to be true based on experience, advice from others, what I've read, and a host of other sources. In relation to what God has called us to do, we are very fortunate that we have the Bible—His Word—and His Holy Spirit. These sources don't provide advice; they provide truth…absolute truth.

When it comes to our calling, we men seem to gain much of our identity from our vocations. Unfortunately, this is never how God planned it to be. Our identity shouldn't come from what we do, but to

Whom we belong. It isn't up to us to come up with or make up what our calling is. We are to seek God's choice. The "what to do" question isn't ours to answer. It's His to tell us. There is no better example for this than how Jesus lived His earthly life.

I was recently providing counsel to a church that had lost its senior pastor. The leadership felt the need to establish a new church focus, which is what we spent much of our time addressing. More specifically, it wasn't what the focus or calling was—it was how to know what it was. Perhaps there are numerous ways to get to the end result, to determine what God's specific calling is for a specific person or church. We do know the answer to one important question though: Does God speak to His people about what He is up to? Yes! "Indeed, the Lord GOD does nothing without revealing His counsel to His servants the prophets" (Amos 3:7). The approach this particular church used to determine God's call was a series of surveys they took over 18 months time. While this method will discover some of the needs in the community, it doesn't necessarily uncover what God wants a church or person to emphasize or accomplish.

Another approach that people fall back on is tradition. "We've been doing it this way, so let's just continue this way." Another method is the "What can I do for God?" or "God needs me to do this for Him" approach. I also call this the "good idea" approach. But does God really need our "good" ideas? "[The LORD says,] My thoughts are not your thoughts, and your ways are not My ways" (Isaiah 55:8). This is similar to going into the woods and telling the animals how I plan to hunt them and expecting them to comply.

God didn't approach Noah and say, "I'm going to flood the earth. You should figure out the best way to keep you and your family from drowning. Oh, and see if you can take care of some animals too." Neither did God tell Moses, "I want to bring My people out of Egypt and into the Promised Land. Figure out who you should talk to about it."

How then should we approach discovering God's will? We can look to no better method than how Christ approached His earthly calling. Jesus did not sit down and strategize how He would spread the gospel. Actually, He also never spoke or did anything on His own accord. He only did what the Father told Him to say and do:

Jesus answered them, "*My teaching* isn't Mine but *is from the One who sent Me*" (John 7:16).

Jesus said to them, "When you lift up the Son of Man, then you will know that I am He, and that *I do nothing on My own*. But just as the Father taught Me, I say these things" (John 8:28).

I have not spoken on My own, but *the Father* Himself who sent Me *has given Me a command as to what I should say and what I should speak* (John 12:49).

Don't you believe that I am in the Father and the Father is in Me? The words I speak to you *I do not speak on My own*. The Father who lives in Me does His works (John 14:10).

Jesus listened and obeyed.

What about our personal involvement in the "doing" of God's will? We are to pick up our crosses:

Jesus said to His disciples, "If anyone wants to come with Me, he must deny himself, take up his cross, and follow Me" (Matthew 16:24).

Whoever does not bear his own cross and come after Me cannot be My disciple (Luke 14:27).

In the same way, therefore, every one of you who does not say good-bye to all his possessions cannot be My disciple (Luke 14:33).

To pick up your cross is not referring to something that involves a bad back, a limp, or even a stuttering problem. No, it's about making the choice to follow what Jesus has called you to do. Regardless of what that is, it will likely be a God-sized calling. I'm not saying it refers to something "big" or "important" in human eyes, such as television, radio, or something that places you in the spotlight. By God-sized I'm referring to a calling that you can only fulfill with God's help. When a task is God-sized, we can't do it on our own, which means we can't steal what belongs to Him—glory and honor. We can't take the credit.

God-sized tasks will likely pull you out of your comfort zone, the place where you feel like you're in control. Hebrews 11:6 has something say about whether our comfort zones please God: "Now without faith it is impossible to please God, for the one who draws near to Him must believe that He exists and rewards those who seek Him."

Being in a place where we are not in control because God is highlights a predicament of our faith. We are challenged to dig deep and decide whether we believe this call is from God. If it is, then it requires action. Henry Blackaby, in his book *Experiencing God,* calls this a "crisis of belief."

James 2:19-20 is oftentimes mistaken as a verse that leads to a works-oriented faith:

> Do I hear you professing to believe in the one and only God, but then observe you complacently sitting back as if you had done something wonderful? That's just great. Demons do that, but what good does it do them? Use your heads! Do you suppose for a minute that you can cut faith and works in two and not end up with a corpse on your hands? (MSG).

What James is really commenting on is separating our faith and our response to our calling. So how do we know what God is calling us to do? There are several components to consider:

- *What does God's Word say?* Look to the Bible for wisdom and guidance.

- *What do our trusted Christian friends and counselors say?* Ask for godly advice based on the Bible and God's principles.

- *What do the circumstances say?* What is God speaking to your heart right now? How can this situation use your spiritual gifts or God-given talents?

"When the Spirit of truth comes, He will guide you into all the truth. For He will not speak on His own, but He will speak whatever He hears. He will also declare to you what is to come" (John 16:13).

This brings to mind something interesting regarding spiritual gifts. I've taken many spiritual gift inventories, and to be honest there have been times when I didn't like the results so I took the assessment again. The second time I skewed the results in a direction more in line with what I thought the results should be. Of course, this is *not* the way to approach these inventories. I've decided that since they tend to be experiential they shouldn't carry much weight. Asking how you feel in or about certain situations isn't a solid base and could keep us from something new God wants to do through us. If we stick only to situations and actions we're comfortable with, it can be very easy to take the credit for the work being done. If the work truly requires a gift I don't possess in my humanness, then I can't take credit for accomplishing the task.

To determine spiritual gifting, let's follow a path that clearly removes us from the driver's seat. Who gives spiritual gifts? The Holy Spirit. "A manifestation of the Spirit is given to each person to produce what is beneficial...But one and the same Spirit is active in all these, distributing to each one as He wills" (1 Corinthians 12:7). The Holy Spirit provides the gifts, but why does He chose the gifts and people He does? Because the Holy Spirit *searches the Father's heart*: "God has revealed them to us by the Spirit, for the Spirit searches everything, even the deep things of God. For who among men knows the concerns of a man except the spirit of the man that is in him? In the same way, no one knows the concerns of God except the Spirit of God" (1 Corinthians 2:10-11).

I was once faced with a decision about whether to oversee a large singles ministry in North Carolina not long after I accepted Christ as my Savior and Lord. For nearly a month I wrestled with it. My thoughts and emotions were all over the place. I was ready, willing, and able to lead the ministry one day. The next, I never wanted to go back there again. Then the next day all I wanted to do was attend the ministry but have nothing to do with leading it. Then I received a call from John Kenline, who worked for Campus Crusade for Christ at the time. He asked how I was doing with the decision. I admitted I was all over the chart. His next question was quite interesting. He asked if I wanted to do God's will no matter what it was. I said yes. John said, "Then don't you think He'll make it hard to get out of His will?"

Imagine that! A God who is interested enough in us to make it easy for us to determine His will.

===================== **YOUR FIELD NOTES** =====================

What decisions have you made in the past when it was difficult to discern God's leading? What were the circumstances and results?

When have you clearly seen God's leading? What were the circumstances and results?

35

Warning!

Several years ago my son Ken and I went for a hike in Rocky Mountain National Park located just west of Estes Park, Colorado. It was late in the day, and the weather was a brisk 25 degrees and windy. We made it to Cub Lake around sunset, and the view was spectacular. In the beauty of this setting, I would soon learn a valuable lesson.

I was wearing several layers to keep warm: a cotton long-sleeve shirt, a cotton sweatshirt, and a nylon shell. Because it was a steady uphill hike, I was hot and very sweaty when we arrived at the lake. The nylon shell had done a great job of keeping the moisture in, so I was soaking wet. I took off the shell to let it dry, and the sweat in my jacket froze immediately.

As I worked on getting dry, in no time at all I got cold—very cold. Remember, it was 25 degrees out, windy, and I was soaking wet— perfect conditions for hypothermia. Hypothermia is when your core body temperature drops below 95 degrees. One way the body responds in the early stages of this condition is to create body heat by shivering. As the hypothermia worsens, the body will, among others things, shiver more violently. Finally the major organs fail in stage three. Hypothermia can be a really sneaky culprit—and deadly.

With the hike back to the truck being downhill, I knew I wouldn't be able to stay warm for very long, so we started back immediately. By the time we made it to the truck, I was extremely cold, stumbling, and my speech was slurred. Praise God that all turned out well! I learned a valuable lesson: Do not wear cotton in high country. It also made me more aware of mortality.

Hypothermia isn't the only thing that can sneak up on us if we're not careful. There is a topic not often discussed—time. Time can slip away very quickly. Demands pull us in all sorts of directions. While some of these demands are worthy of our time, such as work, many are not. All too often our relationships are one of the first things to suffer when we're busy. Let's admit it. Relationships with our spouses, children, and the Lord could be much better than what they are.

Now that my youngest kids—the twins—are older, I take them out hiking and on ATVs for short trips. Simply stopping along the trail to talk and listen can be a teaching moment like no other. No trophy animal can take the place of touching a child's heart. Together my kids and I have watched deer, squirrels, lizards, and a host of birds do what they do. These animals offer terrific illustrations about life principles.

My encounter with hypothermia was a wake-up call on many levels, including taking advantage of the time God gives me on this earth. I encourage you not to let the gift of time get to stage three. It might be too late to bring it back.

In Proverbs 6:6 the obvious topic revolves around laziness: "Go to the ant, you slacker! Observe its ways and become wise." But there is another aspect as well. Did you notice it admonishes us to watch ants? God can, has, and will use nature to speak to us. Let's listen!

YOUR FIELD NOTES

What are some life lessons you've learned while hunting or fishing that you can pass along to your family?

How did these lessons impact your life—and your approach to life?

36

Off the Beaten Path

Brad Pufpaff is a good friend of mine. I've had the privilege of shooting with him in archery tournaments and on hunting trips. Brad is a pro-staffer affiliated with my Backcountry Bowhunting website and organization. He is a fantastic hunter and sportsman. On this particular backcountry elk hunting trip, we were approximately 30 miles north of Pagosa Springs in southern Colorado and five miles from the trailhead. We'd hiked five miles because I couldn't go 5.1 miles.

An interesting thing happened on this trip. It's actually one of the reasons for the tagline to my website BackcountryBowhunting.com: "Off the Beaten Path...No Regrets." We'd been elk calling while hiking along the trail but hadn't heard any responses. When I finally ran out of steam, we tried to call from that location. Still no luck.

We picked our campsite, about 40 yards off the trail, dropped our packs, and made one more estrus cow call. Low and behold, a bull responded—and he sounded close! Fifteen minutes later I had an arrow in a nice 6 x 6!

We spent the next few days hunting near camp to fill Brad's tag. Unfortunately, the huge 350-inch bull I called in for Brad never presented a good shot. At least he was exciting to watch.

Brad and I discovered something very interesting on the hunt. Animals know and care where the trail is. The elk were not pressured where we were, so their activity level and behavior fell within normal range. When we called from the trail or close to it, no elk would respond. If we got off the trail a ways, it was almost routine for numerous bulls to answer. They knew exactly where the trail was! They wouldn't take the bait if we were near the beaten path. Moving 30 to 40 yards away was all we needed to do to get them to answer.

The trail we were on was a main path hunters and outfitters took to get into that area. I've noticed that society seems to be going down a main path too—one going downhill. With more and more social pressure around us, it can be hard to stay on the narrow road described in Matthew 7:13: "Enter through the narrow gate. For the gate is wide and the road is broad that leads to destruction, and there are many who go through it."

Getting off the beaten path the majority of people follow and choosing the clearly defined path the Lord has revealed has proven to be a decision with no regrets for me. It can be the same for you.

YOUR FIELD NOTES

What decisions have you made that were difficult to follow through on but left you with no regrets?

37

Listening

Dove hunting. It's easy, right? Anyway it seems like it ought to be easy enough. All you have to do is hit a little bird as it flies by. Prior to my first venture out to a plowed dove field, a buddy asked me how many boxes of shotgun shells I was planning to take. *Boxes?* I wondered. *Why would I need more than one box? The limit is 15 doves per day, so why would I need more than 25 shells?* Although I may not be the best shot in the world, I consider myself a pretty good one. I didn't expect to fill my limit my first time out, but I did plan on at least bringing enough home for a meal.

As I saw the first dove fly by, I raised my dad's World War II era Winchester Model 12, 16-gauge shotgun, squeezed the trigger. One dove down. One shot, one kill. *Who needs more than one box of shells? Certainly not me!* I thought. Boy, was I ever wrong! It took 24 more shells just to get two more doves that day. *Okay, so maybe I do need more than a single box of shells.* If I'd listened to the wise counsel of my friend who had hunted doves before—who had gone to the fields before me—I would have experienced less disappointment and lengthened my day outdoors.

Scripture is full of examples of the wisdom revealed by people who have gone before us. Proverbs 18:4 sheds light on the richness of good counsel: "The words of a man's mouth are deep waters, a flowing river, a fountain of wisdom." Verse 15 speaks of those who are interested in growing in wisdom: "The mind of the discerning acquires knowledge, and the ear of the wise seeks it."

What about those people who think they know it all? The ones who seem to be experts no matter what the topic is? You know who I'm talking about. People who won't listen to anyone. Proverbs 18:1 has very strong words to say about that type: "One who isolates himself pursues selfish desires; he rebels against all sound judgment."

So let's seek God's wisdom! "The plans of the diligent certainly lead to profit" (Proverbs 21:5). Planning, acquiring wisdom, and discovering insights lead to real blessings. We need to make sure we stay teachable.

YOUR FIELD NOTES

What is the most significant thing you've learned by seeking the counsel of another person? What was the situation and topic?

Who was the person who advised you, and why did you seek him out?

38

Life Is Precious

My father flew cargo planes during World War II. Whenever we were at family reunions, the boys and men would sit and listen to my father tell stories of his days flying over "the Hump" between China and India. We were riveted by the things he experienced as he told stories of triumph, danger, and friends killed in action. Although I would sit and listen for hours to his recollections and hear his heartaches over friends lost, I couldn't fully relate or understand. That is, until I returned home from the 1990 Desert Shield/Desert Storm offensive in Iraq.

The first thing Dad and I had in common in this area was where we both touched down on United States soil when returning home from our wars: Westover, Massachusetts. Another area we have in common is experiencing the death of close friends. I could finally deeply relate to his heartaches. It was quite sobering when my flight crew and I showed up to fly a mission from Thumrait, Oman, to Riyadh, Saudi Arabia, during the war. Our job was to fly the remains of a friend killed three days earlier in the crash of his F-15E Strike Eagle and another serviceman on the first stage of their journey home. My memory of two silver caskets with U.S. flags draped over them sitting in the cargo compartment of a C-130 Hercules is still a reminder that our days are numbered and life is precious.

We all have stories of the people we've known and the events and situations we've experienced in the field and during the daily routines of life. I hope you've used this book to write down your stories so you can pass your legacy on to your children and the following generations. I pray you will continue to jot down your beliefs, thoughts, and ideas and use them to share and start discussions.

And don't forget to share your relationship with Jesus Christ and how you live that out. Your salvation story and spiritual goals can encourage those who follow and even challenge them to walk with Christ. "They conquered [the accuser] by the blood of the Lamb and by *the word of their testimony,* for they did not love their lives in the face of death" (Revelations 12:11).

Feel free to go back in this book and add more comments or even start your own field notes journal. There are sample pages for recording hunting information and your day-to-day thoughts at the end of this book. Feel free to copy them to create your own notebook. The blessings of your experiences and stories—your testimony—to others is immeasurable.

> Love the LORD your God with all your heart, with all your soul, and with all your strength. These words that I am giving you today are to be in your heart. Repeat them to your children. Talk about them when you sit in your house and when you walk along the road, when you lie down and when you get up (Deuteronomy 6:5-7).

Part 3

Your Trail

Your Legacy

We hope you will choose to share with those who love you the most your values, your hopes, your disappointments, your triumphs so they can discover who you are and draw closer to you. All will benefit greatly. Leave a positive legacy.

You Can Do It!

God created you uniquely for a mission. Everything that has occurred in your life has contributed to preparing and equipping you. You have valuable information and life experiences to share! Let those who love you draw strength, encouragement, and wisdom by reading your story and following the ups and downs of your journey. We encourage you to copy the "My Field Notes" and "Hunting Field Notes" pages at the end of this book and create your own journal. For best results, pick a specific time each day to write and answer the questions. Your answers don't need to be lengthy, but the more complete your entry, the more valuable your legacy will be.

God is the author of your life, and you are the storyteller. You can make a difference now and in the years to come. We encourage you to give journaling and sharing a try. You don't have to follow a specific format, make sure everything is spelled correctly, or worry about grammar. Just write what's on your heart and tell what you've experienced. Keep it simple. The goal isn't to write a book. It's to encourage your children and loved ones…to leave a legacy of love for God, for family, for the life we are given in Christ.

Hunting Field Notes

Date of Hunt: Species:

Country: State/Province: Area/Unit:

Harvest: Yes No   Time of Day: Call Used:

Weather: Wind Direction: Moon Phase:

GPS Positions

1: Latitude: Longitude: Elevation: ID:

2: Latitude: Longitude: Elevation: ID:

3: Latitude: Longitude: Elevation: ID:

Equipment

Gun: Model: Caliber: Bullet Wt.:

Bow: Model: Draw Wt.:

Arrow: Model: Length: Wt.:

Hunting Buddies

Name: Phone: Town:

Harvest: Yes No   Time of Day: Call Used:

Name: Phone: Town:

Harvest: Yes No   Time of Day: Call Used:

Name: Phone   Town:

Harvest: Yes No   Time of Day: Call Used:

Memorable Events and Situations

What I Learned on This Trip

What God Revealed and/or My Thoughts

Hunting Field Notes

Date of Hunt: Species:
Country: State/Province: Area/Unit:
Harvest: Yes No   Time of Day: Call Used:
Weather: Wind Direction: Moon Phase:

GPS Positions

1: Latitude: Longitude: Elevation: ID:
2: Latitude: Longitude: Elevation: ID:
3: Latitude: Longitude: Elevation: ID:

Equipment

Gun: Model: Caliber: Bullet Wt.:
Bow: Model: Draw Wt.:
Arrow: Model: Length: Wt.:

Hunting Buddies

Name: Phone: Town:
Harvest: Yes No   Time of Day: Call Used:

Name: Phone: Town:
Harvest: Yes No   Time of Day: Call Used:

Name: Phone   Town:
Harvest: Yes No   Time of Day: Call Used:

Memorable Events and Situations

What I Learned on This Trip

What God Revealed and/or My Thoughts

My Field Notes

What is the best thing that happened in my life today?

What is the worst thing that happened in my life today?

What effort did I make today on behalf of someone else?

Whom do I need to pray for today? What do I need to pray for him or her?

How did I make a difference in somebody's life today?

What did I learn today?

What did God tell me today?

My Field Notes

What is the best thing that happened in my life today?

What is the worst thing that happened in my life today?

What effort did I make today on behalf of someone else?

Whom do I need to pray for today? What do I need to pray for him or her?

How did I make a difference in somebody's life today?

What did I learn today?

What did God tell me today?